FROM THE
RED TEES

FROM THE
RED TEES

HELP, HOPE, AND
HUMOR FOR THE WOMEN
ON THE GREEN

CELESTE PALERMO

CUMBERLAND HOUSE
NASHVILLE, TENNESSEE

FROM THE RED TEES
PUBLISHED BY CUMBERLAND HOUSE PUBLISHING, INC.
431 Harding Industrial Drive
Nashville, TN 37211-3160

The information, etiquette, and rules in this book reflect the game of
golf as understood and communicated by the author. The information
and rules contained herein are the author's interpretation of such,
not official information and *The Rules of Golf* of the USGA/R&A. This
book does not carry the approval or endorsement of the USGA/R&A,
who do not therefore warrant the accuracy of such interpretations.
Readers should refer to official publications of the USGA/R&A for the
complete text of *The Rules of Golf* and other pertinent information
regarding the sport.

Cover design: Gore Studio, Inc.
Text design: John Mitchell

Library of Congress Cataloging-in-Publication Data

Palermo, Celeste, 1972-
  From the red tees : help, hope, and humor for the women on the
green / Celeste Palermo.
      p. cm.
  Includes index.
  ISBN-13: 978-1-58182-588-6 (hardcover : alk. paper)
  ISBN-10: 1-58182-588-9 (hardcover : alk. paper)
  1. Golf–Miscellanea. 2. Golf for women. I. Title.

  GV967.P35 2007
  796.352–dc22

                                                      2007001407

Printed in the United States of America

1 2 3 4 5 6 7—13 12 11 10 09 08 07

For my girls,
Peyton and Morgan,
and
all the women who take a swing
From the Red Tees

CONTENTS

ACKNOWLEDGMENTS

I have a little plaque in my office that says: *She believed she could, so she did.*

I bought the sign at a Hallmark store sometime after I started writing this book, but long before it found a home at Cumberland House. It became a daily reminder to keep working toward a dream.

Now that dream is in your hand, and I have many people to thank—countless friends and acquaintances whose ideas and companionship on the golf course contributed to this book. There are, however, a few individuals whose very hearts and lives are in the fabric of these pages, people who taught me, encouraged me, and supported me.

They believed I could, so we did. I am forever grateful to these special people. They are:

Linda Titcomb, my mom, whose contribution is integral to this work. She spent countless hours editing these pages. She is my trusted counselor, advisor, and friend.

Dan Titcomb, my dad, whose guidance and love shine through each sentence. He has believed in me from first step to first book—and continues to believe.

Cara Maclean, my sister, who has offered constructive input, honest feedback, and hilarious snippets. In every way, she raises the bar of what a sister is and should be.

Jim and Taylor Artman, who have seen the good, the bad, and the very ugly—and still let me play golf with them. They are the true "pros" of the family.

Gayla Artman, Michael Palermo, and Steve and Lori Blackwell, who offer endless encouragement and love. I am so blessed to have them in my life.

Carolyn Drever, Heather Parrish, Erika Wyrick, and Ashley Gehrke, who love me even when I am cranky, forgetful, and way over par. They are all fabulous.

Craig Maclean, Ken Rasbid, Mike Downey, Jason Mannos, Rob Olis, and Chris Minton, who all are true gentlemen and contributed candid feedback and thoughts.

Julie Werking, who provided great tips and fun stories; she is an amazing mom and golfer.

Rick Broadhead, whose efforts on behalf of *From the Red Tees* gave me hope.

Alan Ross, who polished the pages and added expertise as my copy editor.

The team at Cumberland House Publishing: Ron Pitkin, Stacie Bauerle, John Mitchell, Andrea Davis, and Mike Middleton, who all embraced my vision for *From the Red Tees*. I appreciate their expertise and hard work in bringing this book to fruition.

Peyton and Morgan Palermo, my daughters, whose curiosity, vibrancy, and enthusiasm for life are my constant inspiration. The energy with which they explore the world amazes me.

And finally, Pete Palermo, my husband, who has kept my clubs clean through it all. I love you. You are a wonderful golfer, partner, father, and friend.

INTRODUCTION

"Golf is like a love affair.
If you don't take it too seriously, it's no fun;
if you do take it seriously, it breaks your heart."

— Arnold Daly

IT'S ABOUT TIME I broke a hundred," I say to my husband as we drive home from the golf course.

"Why do you say that?" he asks.

"Well, I've been playing nine years. I'm due, don't ya think?"

"You haven't really been *playing*," he says.

"Yes, I have."

"People who *play*, play all the time," he continues. "You golfed, what … two times last year?"

"More than that."

"When?"

I rattle off my rounds for the previous year.

"OK, four times," he says. "You don't *play* golf."

Ever since meeting my husband, in the spirit of shared interest and mutual recreation, I have attempted to golf. It's been a long road filled with more frustration and humiliation than I care to remember. Learning the game in the presence of my husband, his family, and our friends has proven to be quite humbling. I have been confused by the terminology, shamed by my inconsistency, and accused of having "seizures" on the putting green. I have had a complete breakdown in a bunker and made a hole-in-one, only to shank my keepsake ball into a water hazard on the next hole. Still, I keep coming back. Through it all, I have steadily improved my game and developed a genuine interest in the sport. Now, I *play* regularly—with my husband, with friends, and in a women's league.

And I'm not alone. There are so many women on the course these days. I see you, with your husbands, boyfriends, and friends, playing for fun. I see you with clients, trying to improve a business relationship or attempting the game because a pal talked you into it. We are out there, and yet so many of us start out lacking knowledge of the basics and consistent exposure to the game. I never picked up a club or set foot on a golf course until I met my husband. A "driver" to me was the capped gentleman who drives the limo to the prom. Pathetic? Maybe, but I'm willing to bet many of you are in the same boat.

Well, whatever your reason for being on the links, if you're going to play, you may as well know your stuff. This would be a good time for me to disclose that I am not a golf professional—or maybe you've already guessed that. I don't know every rule in the Big Book of Golf, but I know the basics. And I've learned the hard way. I am just like you. I started out a little (OK, a lot) green behind the ears and have learned what to do—and what not to do—through lots of golf, lots of mistakes, lots of frustration, and lots of lessons. I know what you need to know to feel comfortable and have more fun on the golf course, whether it's your first round or you play the game on a regular basis.

This is the book I looked for when I started. I'll share all the things I've learned in nine years of observing, attempting, and *playing* the game.

I have done the research. I have recorded countless humiliations (my own) and eavesdropped on many post-round conversations in the clubhouse. I have also researched the rules, chatted up golf professionals on what really matters, and taken notes on the course. These notes, scribbled frantically with a dull, three-inch golf pencil in a bouncy cart as my partner drove to each hole, were, at times, incredibly hard to decipher. But they are, nonetheless, great notes.

My hope in writing this book is that you'll be better informed, feel more confident, and have more fun on the links. By the time you turn the last page, you'll be in the know. Others will have more fun playing with you because you "know" the basics of the game. I hope you will heed my advice, avoid my mistakes, and quickly advance in your game. I hope you learn a lot, laugh a bunch—and that I see you playing *From the Red Tees* very soon.

Good Luck!

— CP

FROM THE
RED TEES

WOMEN ON THE GREEN

It's Par for the Course

*May thy ball lie in green pastures
—and not in still waters.*

— Anonymous

T HE DAY IS perfect. The sky is ice blue without a cloud on the horizon. The wind dances through the palm trees whispering quietly, the gentle rustle reminiscent of soft rainfall. Only the faint hum of a distant airplane breaks the reverie. This is good; this is very good. Today I will shoot my best round yet.

I tee up my ball and take my stance, stepping like a nervous horse. I look over my left shoulder toward the pin and fix my aim. I set my grip, drop my shoulders, and E-X-H-A-L-E. *Ahhhh.*

Arms straight. Don't stand up. Keep your eye on the ball. A litany of tips runs through my head. *Don't try to kill it. Just swing, nice and easy.* I send positive affirmations into the universe, like Stuart Smalley: *I'm good enough, I'm strong enough, and doggone it, I can hit this ball. I'm a great golfer. The entire fairway is mine. Watch me now. I can feel it—this is going to be the drive of the day.*

I have blocked all distractions and ignore the three people staring at me, waiting for me to swing. All is well with the world. It is time.

I swing.

Whoosh.

My eyes are looking to see where the ball has gone, and yet the ball—that damned ball— still sits untouched on the tee.

I can feel the heat in my cheeks. It's not sunshine giving me the unfavorable burn, it is shame. In an instant, I'm the girl picked last, the player nobody wants. I suck. Voices taunt me: *Why are you even here? Who are you trying to fool? You'll never be any good at this game. Why try? You're making an idiot of yourself.*

I can't look at my husband and his two friends standing behind me. I rationalize that, depending on the angle, my whiff might have looked like a practice swing. I feel a little better hiding behind this charade. I focus forward, knowing that if they see the frustration on my face, they'll know the truth.

"You stood up." My husband's all-knowing voice breaks the silence.

Damn. My rationalizations vanish along with my pride. Oh well, it can't get much worse. I reset my grip on the driver and take an angry hack. Who cares about this game, anyway?

Smack.

I look up to see my little white ball sailing through the sky like a 747 jumbo jet. It makes a perfect approach and lands in the middle of the fairway, rolling straight toward the green, just past my husband's ball.

I'm not the uncoordinated class loser! Oh no! I am Michelle Wie! I am Annika Sorenstam! I love the game of golf! I have redeemed myself. There is hope for me yet.

I pick up my tee and head back to the cart, smiling as if in a speed round of mood schizo-phrenia.

"Nice hit, Honey. You're laying two."

Laying two. I hate that. My husband's score-keeping reminds me that Michelle and Annika would not have missed the ball on the first swing—and they'd have hit an iron—and they'd be 100 yards past my drive. I hate this sport.

WHY PLAY?

Who knew the nervous, vulnerable feelings one could have learning to play golf among established golfers, most of them men? Who knew how it would feel to be judged, criticized, and humiliated when the stroke count passed double par or when failing even to make contact with that pesky, irritating little ball? Who knew how much time would be involved finding (and begging) a babysitter to watch the kids for the five-plus hours required to play? Who would want to spend their extra money on greens fees and collared shirts when, for the same investment, one could score a stylish Coach purse? Why not take a yoga class, grab a latte and go shopping? Why submit to relentless frustration and humiliation on the golf course when you could be poolside with a good book? Why play the game? Why?

I play golf because I love it. I love the challenge. I love the outdoors and the fresh air. I play because golf takes me out of my comfort zone: I am learning and growing and—despite the frustration, embarrassment, and steep learning curve—having fun. Golf can be as addictive as a high school boyfriend; you know it is likely to make you feel stupid, and your time might be better spent elsewhere, but the challenge and the allure bring you back. And it gets better. I usually see improvement in my game with every round, and this brings me back as well. I play because, as a business-woman, as a mom, as a wife … as a girl, it's Par for the Course.

PAR FOR THE COURSE
Women are taking up golf at a higher rate than men. Why? We play to enhance business relationships, to build friendships, for the athletic challenge, and for the pure release and recreation the sport provides. Really, we're naturals for the game; we possess numerous qualities that can make us better than average golfers.

OK, now that I have your attention, I'll also say this: Most of us also have qualities that could make us horrible golfers, unbearable to play with. Sorry, but it's true. We can be too chatty, overscheduled, and insecure. For the benefit of our game, we must learn to maximize our advantages and eliminate the negatives. Let's tackle the yucky stuff first.

Women love to talk. During the course of the game we can find ourselves chatting about what club to hit, how nervous we are, the weather, what we did last night, and what we had for breakfast. We talk about anything and everything. While this is perfect over coffee at Starbucks, it is not acceptable on the golf course. Here's why:

It contributes to slow play. Slow play is the No. 1 irritant for other golfers, giving us girls a bad rap and contributing to the *women are slow golfers* stereotype.

It hinders our own game. If we're engrossed in what Sheila said to Rick, we can't possibly be paying adequate attention to our game strategy. (Strategy? you ask. Oh, yes, there's strategy involved. Just wait. We'll get there.)

It is discourteous and distracting. Conversing when a fellow golfer is hitting, putting, or

God forbid, teeing off, is just plain rude. Most golfers take their game seriously, and all pay a pretty penny to be putting on the green. Chitchat on the course disrespects their game and yours.

Girl talk is better saved for the post-round happy hour in the clubhouse. Men don't tend to talk as much—they don't rehash the hash browns from breakfast—or talk about much of anything, for that matter. And, in this one instance, that's a good thing. We need to follow their quiet lead here, ladies.

Another factor that can hinder our game is that we tend to overschedule ourselves. My husband will leave any chore undone, pass on any party, and forgo almost anything if given the opportunity to play golf. Most men are similar in their prioritizing/schedule-clearing ability. Women are usually committed to some mandatory lunch meeting, baby shower, or community project when the opportunity for golf rolls around. It's much more difficult to skip out on a bridal shower than to TiVo a basketball game; hence, our overcommitment to other things can hinder our advancement to the Pro Tour.

An overbooked calendar makes it hard to find time to play. No time = No practice. No practice = No progress. If you want to excel at golf, or even make a respectable appearance, you must practice and play on a regular basis.

Our friends are also busy. If they don't have the time for golf, it may be hard to find friends who understand and support your commitment to play. If you feel you have no one to play with, you may be more easily dissuaded and distracted by other endeavors.

The third characteristic that threatens our game is insecurity. If "cut" and "draw" define craft activities with your toddler and "hook" and "bite" are only fishing terms you've heard your husband use, then it's easy to see where a little insecurity might manifest with regard to golf.

If you didn't grow up with the game, you probably lack knowledge. If you recently started playing or do not get sufficient practice time, you likely lack skill. Lack of knowledge and skill leads to insecurity. You must overcome insecurity and silence the golf saboteur. Here's why:

When we're insecure, we can be chatty or

make excuses for our mistakes. Both annoy other golfers.

When we're insecure, we may query others about our game. This is not only distracting, but certain questions—such as, "What club should I hit?"—are not allowed during play. Besides, no partner wants to spend the day hearing, "What am I doing wrong?"

If you feel insecure, it can limit your game. Golf is a mental game—yes, sometimes I think we're mental for playing it—but most of the battle is in your head. A lack of confidence will result in a poor score. Play with confidence!

Overcome insecurity and gain confidence by setting priorities and developing the qualities that make (potentially) fantastic golfers. Remember: Maximize the good, eliminate the bad.

WOMEN OF MANY LEVELS

Now for the fun stuff. Women are hardworking, strategic, cool under pressure, and have big-picture perspective. We can multitask. The same qualities that make us an ace in the boardroom contribute to our ace on the course. Here's why:

Women are hardworking. When we're single or childless, we manage full-time careers, volunteer in the community, organize events with friends, clean our homes, balance our checkbooks and finances, exercise, grocery shop and cook, babysit for friends, clean our cars, do thoughtful things for our partners, plan vacations, manage family relations, and more. If we have a husband and/or kids, then we do all the above and in addition change diapers, visit the pediatrician, supervise school projects, plan balanced meals, make more runs to the store, and do laundry, laundry, laundry, laundry. This propensity for hard work serves us well, as learning golf is no Pop Tart breakfast. It requires regular practice and knowing the rules. A great golf game does not just happen; you must develop it and be willing to make the sacrifices to do so.

Women are strategists. What gal hasn't plotted how to entice an attractive man to buy her a drink or picked out the perfect dress to maximize her assets? A friend of mine planned her pregnancy so the birth would coincide with her spring break from teaching. Golf also takes strategy: What club do you hit? Which way will the ball break? How much should you compensate for wind? These decisions all involve strategy, but there's more. We must strategize how to fit practice—lessons and the driving range—as well as actual rounds into our schedule. Let's face it, when it comes to finesse and finagling the details, we women can only benefit on the links.

Women are cool under pressure. Who gets their gym shorts in a knot when the remote control won't work? Whose life is ruined when their college football team loses a game? Who freaks when there is a sticky substance on the kitchen floor? It isn't us gals. Women are generally more patient and less easily frustrated by the messy details of life. We handle missing remotes, football losses, and spills ... and we can handle the learning curve of golf. The bad swings, the horrible holes, and the terrible rounds are all part of coping with the unexpected disappointments and disasters of life and motherhood.

Women have perspective. When you are used to computer crashes, crayon art on the walls, and a pile of laundry the size of Mount Rainier, then a poor hit (or several) doesn't rattle you. Golf is what it is: a break from the daily routine—the deadlines, dust, and diapers. We know we'll survive even if we shoot (way) over par because we know a bad day of golf always beats a good day of laundry.

Women know how to multitask. This quality is decidedly *not* helpful if we are chatting with our cart mate while contemplating what to make for dinner. It *is* helpful if we apply the skill to our game. If we drive the cart, scan the rough for our friend's lost ball, and contemplate our next hit all in one synaptic snap, then it is advantageous. Successful golf requires focus. The ability to engage in golf-focused multitasking can help improve your game and may even speed up your round.

THE TEE-BOX ADVANTAGE

Playing from the front (red) tees helps women excel at golf. Depending on the course, the red tees may be significantly forward of the men's tee box. Still, on average, most women do not possess the strength and drive distance of most men, so it is logical that we have this advantage. I do not have a powerhouse swing, but on many holes, if I hit the ball solidly, I can outdrive my husband, thanks to the tee-box advantage. He can hit the ball farther on the rest of the fairway, but on the majority of holes, I can still hang with the boys from tee to green. Consider the following scenario:

The hole is a par-4, dogleg left. My husband is 404 yards out, from his tee box to the green. He hits his driver, and his ball goes quite far, disappearing into the tall grass left of the fairway. The distance from my tee box to the pin is 337; meaning I have a 67-yard advantage off the tee box. I hit my driver about 150 yards and plop my ball smack into the middle of the fairway.

My husband's ball is somewhere in the lateral vicinity of mine, but he can't find it. He must take a penalty stroke. He drops his ball, then hits an iron short of the green. He is laying three. I hit my ball again, using a 3-wood, and land about 70 yards out, laying two.

My husband chips up and one-putts for bogey. I hit my 7-iron onto the green and one-putt for par. Wahoo! *Though typically I two-putt and we would have tied the hole, this illustrates my point: Men usually hit the ball farther off the tee, but the farther they hit, the less control they may have. (I'm referring to your average Joe, not a professional player.) I can't hit as far, but my ball generally goes straighter.*

Utilize the driving range to maximize this tee-box advantage. Learn to hit the ball consistently. Of course we all have poor shots now and then, but you *will* improve with practice!

NERVES AND PERSPECTIVE

Speaking of poor shots, what is it about having an audience that renders one unable to make contact with the ball? Why is it that the cute golf pro you've been hoping would ask you out is within eyeshot when you are teeing off the first hole? Why does the clubhouse restaurant (which is *always* packed) overlook the 18th fairway and putting green— so that everyone, ice-cold beer in hand, can watch you, sunburned and dog-tired, try to finish off your round with painful dignity? Why do you always swing and miss (for the first time in months) when you play with your

boss and coworkers? Why is golf—a sport supposedly relaxing and serene—akin to death by
humiliation?

Call it nerves, Murphy's Law, or the devil's
muse, it's a fact: The more people watching, the
worse you will play. It totally sucks to make an
ass of yourself in front of a crowd, but does it
really matter?

I find the best way to cope with these situations is just to play my game. It comes back to
perspective. I am not Michelle Wie; I'm a busy
mom with a career and two kids. If I shank a hit,
so what? I take a deep breath, remind myself I
do not get paid to play golf, and move on.

There is something to be said for women
who refuse to let fear sideline them from life.
This applies to golf. So why don't more women
play? Usually for one of several reasons: They
lack opportunity, they lack funds, they would
rather do something else, or they are afraid—
afraid of looking incompetent, afraid they'll feel
like an idiot, or afraid to become part of what
many deem a "Boys Club."

Some women may say they are too busy—
and some are. Yet how many of us who are "too
busy" or "can't afford it" have husbands who

play golf on a regular basis? If your husband or partner is not too busy and can afford to play, then you also should be able to find the time and the means. Are you watching the kids so he can play every Saturday? Then get him to take the kids on Sunday afternoon.

There is a middle ground; find it. He should respect your request and may even appreciate your budding interest in the sport. If you really don't care to play, pursue something else, but don't sit on the sidelines of life hiding behind excuses. If you try something new, you probably won't be a gold-medal contender the first year. Life is meant

Why Play?

1. Athletic challenge
2. Release and recreation
3. Enhance relationships
4. Outdoor opportunity
5. Comfort-zone buster
6. Nix perfection
7. Muscles were made to be flexed
8. Pushing your limits is a good thing
9. Even though there's always "next time," DON'T WAIT!
10. Mistakes provide a great chance to learn

to be lived, so get out there and take a swing! If you miss the ball, ask yourself:

- Am I playing in the last round of the U.S. Women's Open?
- Am I being graded on my performance by a callous, unsympathetic college professor?
- Will people like me less if I whiff the ball?
- Does this change who I am as a person?

No! No! No! Everyone has bad shots sometimes. All of us make mistakes and can learn from them. If you are missing the ball every time you swing, you may want to visit the driving range for a few lessons and some practice before your next round—for peace of mind and sheer enjoyment of the game. Either way, stand tall. If you swing and miss again, remind yourself:

- It's OK. I'm learning (and everyone makes mistakes).
- I shouldn't expect perfection. I don't play enough to be this hard on myself.
- If I allow a bad hit to ruin my day, what does that say about my life and value system?
- At least I'm trying, pushing my limits, and learning new skills in order to grow.
- I'll do better next time.

Whatever you do, don't become an emotional wreck. Don't cry or huff away—nobody wants to spend the day with a sore loser or a cranky bitch. Shake it off. Maintain perspective. Some people will never get the chance to even try golf … and no matter how poorly you play, it's better than domestic drudgery!

Women on the Green are Par for the Course. You have every right to be on the links, and if, like me, you've been cooped up with paperwork, deadlines, lists, and laundry, you could use some fresh air and exercise. So tee it up and give the game your best shot. Par is in your future!

Keep Two Balls in Your Pocket
Preparedness

*They say golf is like life, but don't believe them.
Golf is more complicated than that.*

— Gardner Dickinson

TAKE A MULLIGAN," says my husband after I fail to clear a pond off the tee box. "Do you have another ball?"

"No."

"Here." He tosses me a ball and I hit again, this time just barely clearing the water and bouncing my ball up onto the fairway.

Later in the round, the wind picks up and I start to sneeze. Ugh! It's an allergy attack. I have no tissues with me, and after a few holes I'm miserable, sniffing every few seconds to fend off—well, I'll spare you the details. I can't focus on my game; I'm thinking only of how to clear my stuffy nose. I rummage in the cart for extra napkins, finding none. I consider taking the cart to the clubhouse bathroom, but this will take too much time away from my game. A farmer blow is *not* an option. So finally, when my husband is yards away taking a shot, I blow my nose into the golf towel hanging on the back of my bag. Sick. I am totally grossed out but relieved at the same time. I make a mental note to put a small pack of tissues and some allergy tablets in my golf bag and then run up to join my group.

My ball is in the line of another player's putt. "Can you mark that, please?" he asks.

"Sure," I say. "Um, Pete, do you have a marker?"

My husband shakes his head and tosses me a dime. I mark my ball.

"My skort doesn't have pockets," I explain as we drive to the next tee box.

"You need pockets," he says. "You have to be prepared or you'll hold up the game for everyone."

"I know," I say. That morning I had debated

with myself and "cute" won out over "practical." But the skort proved to be a poor choice—and I wasn't looking so cute blowing my nose on a muddy golf towel anyway.

Do I sound lame? I felt lame. Preparedness is one of the most important considerations in golf. As a new golfer, you may not always be able to control whether your shot hits the fairway or your putt drops into the cup, but you can always be prepared. Taking time to make sure you're prepared before a round will help you be more comfortable on the course when pollen abounds. It will also help keep up the pace of play, show that you know what you're doing, and demonstrate respect for other golfers.

WHAT TO WEAR

When you call to reserve a tee time, ask about the dress code. Dress codes will vary from place to place, but most courses and clubs require a collared shirt, and denim is not permissible. If you are unfamiliar with what to wear, the best thing to do is call ahead and clarify what attire is appropriate. That said, here are some general guidelines:

Shirts. A collared shirt is standard. You may go sleeveless, short sleeve, or long sleeve, depending on the weather. A soft cotton Polo or a dri-weave fabric that wicks away perspiration is a smart choice. A few women's golf shirts have no collar, but again, it will depend on the rules for each course—even if it is a "golf" shirt— whether you may wear it. Light-colored tops help reflect the sun on hot days; dark colors hide the ketchup drip from your hot dog on the 10th hole.

Shorts/pants, etc. You may wear whatever type of shorts/pants/capris you want with a few considerations. As mentioned before, no denim. Your pants should have pockets big enough to hold an extra golf ball, tees, and a ball marker. Don't wear anything super short; mid-thigh or knee length is a must. I know some women who have worn skirts, but I don't recommend this. I'd worry about flashing the other players in my group when bending down to tee up my ball, and quite frankly, I don't need any distractions from my game. (If your strategy is to distract other players, then perhaps wearing a skirt might work!) One last thought: If "Aunt Flo" is in town, wear dark-colored shorts.

Bathrooms are scarce around most courses, and wearing white could invite a repeat of a junior high disaster.

Shoes. When you're first learning, you may play in tennis shoes. Most public courses allow them, but some clubs require golf shoes, so again, it's always wise to check the dress code. When you buy golf shoes, select some that are comfortable and in a neutral color so they will coordinate with a variety of outfits. Most golf shoes these days have soft spikes, but if you have hard spikes, make sure the course you are playing allows them.

Socks. There are no specific rules. You may wear whatever you want, from argyle knee-highs to white peds. I prefer a short sock, just under my ankle. I hate sock lines and these work best for me. I suggest finding a style you like and tucking an extra pair into your golf bag. I've worn flip-flops to the course and then forgotten to bring socks. You can usually buy a pair at the course, but it's better to be prepared and save your money.

Bra. I suggest wearing a comfortable bra with good support. A sports bra or properly fitting cotton bra are good choices, saving potential pain and embarrassment on the links. It is no fun to have an underwire digging into your chest halfway through your round or to— *Surprise!*—have your bra flip up over your breasts on a hard-hit tee shot. (It happens.)

Glove. Many people wear a golf glove to help grip the club. Gloves come in various sizes and styles. If you wear a glove, make sure it fits properly and is not too tight. Some gloves are available with a snap-on ball marker; this is helpful if, like me, you some-times forget to carry one. Some women's gloves are made without fingers; this style is nice, as it is a bit cooler and you can show off a great manicure! (When it's really hot, my hand sweats in the glove, so I bring two gloves and alternate them throughout the day, Velcro-ing the one I'm not wearing to the bar on the front of my golf cart.)

Golf gloves get nasty quickly. If you cram one into the side pocket of your golf bag post round, it'll look quite gross when you retrieve it the next time—like an old washcloth that has dried into a crunchy wad in your laundry pile. Believe me, you won't want to put your hand in *that*. Yuck. My advice: Once your glove is more brownish than whitish, toss it and ante up for a new one.

Sun protection. No one needs sun-damaged skin. Without proper sun protection, you will be red and wrinkly in short order. The following items are a must:

Hat or visor: Light colors are better than dark if it is a hot day. Hats offer more protection for the top of your head but are more apt to leave you with a sweaty hat-head by the end of your round. A visor provides some protection for your face, but you'll want to dab sunscreen onto the part in your hair to protect the top of your head. With hats and visors, unless you're wearing a bucket hat, remember to put sunscreen on your ears, a common place for skin cancer to occur. (And though few women are bald, it's best to remember—or remind those who are follicly challenged—that visors are not always a great choice. I've seen bald men wearing visors on the course and it just makes me wonder.)

Sunglasses: Sunglasses are a must. Don't buy cheap ones, as UV protection for your eyes is extremely important. If you are playing later in the day, bring the case for your sunglasses and put them away when you no longer need them. I often prop my glasses on the brim of my hat where they tend to fall onto the ground when I'm putting. I've also thrown them into the front of my cart, only to have them blow away somewhere on the course. Bring the case and take care of them.

Sunscreen: You shouldn't play golf without sunscreen any more than you should spend a sunny day on the beach without it. I suggest applying sunscreen on all exposed areas of your body before you get to the course. (Don't forget the back of your legs; I always do, and a sunburn there hurts!) Keep a quality sunscreen in your golf bag in case you need to reapply during the round. I am fair-skinned and always reapply sunscreen after the front nine. Warning: Be careful when applying sunscreen during the course of play; you don't want your hands to be slippery with lotion when you're swinging a club!

Make sure to periodically check the expiration date on your sunscreen. Sunscreen loses its effectiveness over time, and it's extremely frustrating to lube up and still burn. Your game is likely all the frustration you'll need for the day anyway!

WHAT TO BRING

You will not need to bring a ton of stuff to the golf course, but be sure you have all necessary items for the day. Leave your purse and all nonessentials in the trunk; stick your ID, cash, and a credit card in your golf bag. Leave all other valuables at home. I suggest keeping your golf bag organized, with specific pockets for certain items; that way you'll know where something is when you need it. Consider carrying these items:

Golf balls, tees, ball marker, and a divot repair tool. Extra golf balls are a must. Pro shops will sell balls, but you will pay a premium and they may not carry the type you like to hit. Plan ahead and bring extras with you. Also, many courses will provide tees, but bring your own, just in case. A dime or small coin can be used as a ball marker—and a divot repair tool is a great inexpensive item to keep in your bag as well.

Golf glove. I sometimes bring several.

Golf shoes, extra socks. I keep these in my golf bag; that way I always have them.

Windbreaker/rain jacket with a hood. It's a good idea to keep a light jacket in your golf bag; you never know when a storm might blow in. As with my shoes, I leave this in my bag so I have it at all times.

Umbrella. If the weather looks blustery, you might toss a wooden-shaft umbrella in with your clubs. However, I've never used an umbrella when golfing. First of all, you can't hold an umbrella and swing at the same time, but that's not the main reason. If the weather looks like it will pass quickly and there is no thunder, I usually grab my hooded windbreaker and keep playing, but if there is *any* lightning or thunder, I call it a day. Use common sense. You don't want to be out on the course in a thunderstorm, umbrella or not. If a storm rolls in, head for cover and try to get a rain check. Don't risk your life for a round of golf.

Money. You may use a credit/debit card to pay for your round and pro shop purchases, but be sure to carry enough cash for the beverage cart, tips for the bag boys, etc.

Sunscreen, lip protection, a tampon, tissues, a ponytail elastic. Keep all these common-sense items in your bag. You'll be glad you did!

Medicines. If you are prone to allergy attacks, as I am, you may want to keep allergy medicine in your bag. If you have asthma, bring your inhaler. Bring pain reliever medication and a Band-Aid, just in case you get a frustration headache or a blister.

Snacks. If you tend to get hungry during play and a Snickers and beer are not your idea of a healthy snack, you might want to bring one. Dried fruit, nuts, and granola bars are good suggestions. Stay away from anything that might melt, such as chocolate, and anything that will spoil. A friend of mine put a pear in her golf bag and then forgot about it until her next round several months later when her fingers sank into the squishy, rotten mess as she reached in her bag to find a ball. Sick!

Miscellaneous. You may want to bring a cell phone (with the ringer set on vibrate!), just in case your cart dies or you need to check in with the babysitter. I also like to carry a small USGA rule book, for those times when I'm unsure how to play a certain ball. And certainly stash a copy of *From the Red Tees* in your bag for good measure and quick reference.

It's a good idea to clean out your golf bag occasionally, removing unnecessary items and restocking what you need. I just checked the contents of my bag and found three lip glosses, a ring, and a pair of hoop earrings I thought I'd lost. I also discovered a rank pair of socks. Good thing I checked!

WHAT NOT TO WEAR/BRING

Some of this is common sense, but you'd be surprised what people wear and bring to the golf course. Let's go over the basics:

Don't wear crazy fashion-statement outfits. This will just draw (negative) attention to you. When dressing for the course, think classy and sporty, function over fashion. (Once you make the LPGA tour, you can wear whatever you want. Many professionals, such as the late Payne Stewart, have a signature style.) As a novice golfer, be wary of crazy clothes, funky hats, and bug-eyed glasses.

Don't wear lots of jewelry. Leave your rings, necklaces, and bracelets at home. (If you forget to do so and they bother you while playing, take them off and tuck them into your golf bag, but remember to remove them later.) I don't wear my wedding ring—or any other rings—when I play golf, as they feel lumpy under my golf glove.

Leave your purse in the car and your valuables at home. Figure out what you really need, and tuck only those items into your golf bag. Think nomad; travel light.

BEFORE YOU PLAY

Arrive early. Plan to get to the course 30 to 45 minutes before your tee time. You don't want to be rushed, and you'll need time to check in and pay, load your clubs onto the cart, and get refreshments. You'll also want some time to warm up. It's a good idea to stretch out and practice your swing.

I like to get a bucket of balls and spend at least 15 minutes on the driving range before I play a round. Usually I select the clubs I use most and hit several shots with each one. The clubs you like best will vary; I prefer to warm up with my driver, my 3-wood, a 5- and 7-iron, and my pitching wedge.

After that, I practice putting. Greens will vary from course to course, and it's good to get a read on how putts will roll before you start to play. Good putting is as important (or more so) than a good drive, as putts add up quickly. If you have time, work on your chip shot. Then:

Go to the bathroom. You'll be glad you did.

If you haven't eaten, get some food. Don't depend on the beverage and snack cart for sustenance. (Low blood sugar and dizziness are not good for your health or your game.)

Check that your bag is well secured to the cart. Also make sure all zippers and pockets are closed. You don't want your bag to fall off and scatter personal items along the fairway.

Arrive at the start on time. Also make sure you're warmed up, focused, and ready to play.

ON THE COURSE

There are a few things to remember when on the course. Among the more important are:

Be sure to stay hydrated. If you don't have to pee during the course of your game, you aren't drinking enough liquids. Also remember that alcohol is a diuretic, so if you drink a beer, you'll need to consume even more water to compensate. Do I sound like a mom, nagging about food and adequate fluids? Well, I *am* a mom, and this stuff is crucial.

At the start of the round, put two balls, two tees, a ball marker, and a divot repair tool in your pocket. This way, when you tee off, if you shank a shot and take a mulligan or want to hit again, you won't waste time going back to the cart for another ball. Likewise, keep an extra tee handy in case you break one. If you have a dime or some other ball marker in your pocket at the start of the game, you'll be ready when you need to mark your ball later in the round.

When it's your turn to tee off, be ready. Don't watch the other players hit and then go to the cart for your club; have it in your hand. If you and your boyfriend are playing with another couple and the guys hit first, watch them tee off, then drive to your tee. Both girls should select a club and go up to the tee box together. Do not sit in the cart watching and then get your club. Stand back from whoever hits first and wait your turn. Speed of play is key. Likewise, on the fairway, when your partner goes to hit her ball, you should go to yours.

But first, make sure it's safe, that you aren't in the "line of fire" of someone else's shot, then grab the club you need and walk to your ball. If you're not sure which club to take, grab a few that you might use, then when you get to your ball, choose the appropriate club. This way, as soon as your partner hits, you can hit. You must be aware, be prepared, and use time efficiently on the course. This is vital to pace of play.

THE DRIVING RANGE

Practice is part of preparation. If you can get to the driving range on a regular basis, it will help your game immensely. Here are some helpful hints:

Take all your clubs, wear your golf shoes, and get a bucket of practice balls. At most ranges you can rent a bucket of practice balls in the pro shop; at others, after you pay, you'll be given a token for a ball machine. This works like an ice machine—just put the bucket under the dispenser and press the button. At many ranges you can purchase either a small or large bucket of balls; be sure to place the right size bucket under the dispenser. Everyone likes a jackpot in Vegas, but if you purchase a large bucket and put a small bucket under the dispenser, your jackpot will be more embarrassing and harder to contain. If you're unsure where the ball machine is located, or if you have other questions, just ask.

Put tees in your pocket so you can practice hitting your driver. Always be alert and aware on the driving range. Don't walk too closely to anyone; serious injury may result from getting hit in the head with a golf club. Find an open spot (or wait until there is one) and then set your clubs down and get to work.

Silence is key. If you go to the driving range with a friend, refrain from chitchatting while you hit, as many people are concentrating and idle talk is distracting. Just take your stance in the middle area (it's usually marked) and start to practice.

Practice hitting all the clubs in your bag. Don't just hit your driver. When I first started going to the range, I would usually hit my 3-wood and my driver pretty well but have less success with my irons. As a result, I'd only hit the 3-wood and driver. Doing this built my confidence and made me feel like a great golfer, but I fell apart on the course. So hit the clubs you use most frequently, but also hit the ones with which you need the most practice. Ideally, you should hit all your clubs several times. When you've hit the same club several times with consistent distance and loft, move on to another club.

Pay attention. The benefit of the driving

range is not only learning how to hit your clubs consistently but also increasing how far you can hit each club. As you prepare to strike each ball, look at the pins and make a mental note of where they are (they'll be marked). Aim. After you hit, watch where your ball lands and estimate the distance. Everyone hits their clubs differently, so it's important for you to know how far you can hit with each of your clubs.

There's a par-3 at my home course that is 136 yards to the pin. On this hole I always hit my driver off the tee box. It may sound like way too much club, but with the slope of the terrain and the amount of brush surrounding the area, I need the distance and the loft of my driver. For many people, a driver is *way* too much club, but for me, it's perfect. I usually land the ball right next to the pin. I've had several birdies on this hole. If I were to use the same club other players hit, I would fall short or land in the gunch. Golf is an individual game. The driving range is the perfect place to assess your capabilities and find out what works for you. Apply this knowledge on the course.

To make the driving range interesting, some people target the caged cart that periodically circles collecting practice balls. I've never hit the cart, and maybe the driver appreciates that fact. More likely, I'd hit the beverage cart out on the open course even when trying to avoid it. Golf is a sport full of "ironies," so I am particularly careful to avoid hitting objects and people at all times.

Speaking of targets, no one likes to be an unsuspecting target on any occasion. As a woman at the driving range, however, you may be. Nobody will aim their swing at you, of course, but some men may take their chances just to see if you are in the field of play, so to speak. I have had men hit on me at the range; you may too. If you find a "helpful gentleman" critiquing your swing, use your best judgment on the advice. If you're single and he's the cute golf pro you've been eyeing, take the tip and his number. If not, politely thank the gentleman, letting him know you'd rather hit practice balls than chat. He should get the hint.

LESSONS

If you're serious about your game, lessons are a valuable option. A professional instructor should be able to pinpoint the parts of your game that need the most work. Concentrate on those areas. Lessons combined with regular practice should facilitate rapid improvement, taking strokes off your score every time you play.

Lessons are available through a variety of sources and locations. Costs will vary depending on the facility, the number of lessons, and whether you are taking private, semi-private, or group instruction. Most all clubs and courses have on-site professionals who offer lessons. Many colleges and community recreation centers also offer lessons, and golf stores often have contact information for local professionals. With a few phone calls or Internet research, you should be able to locate and price out a few options that will work for you.

Keep in mind that if you have a busy schedule, private lessons might better accommodate you, but they will be more expensive. Likewise, group lessons through a recreation center or local college may only be offered at certain times but could be much less expensive. If you're looking for a female instructor, it may take more legwork. Women pros are out there, but they may be harder to find.

OTHER RESOURCES

Here are a few other ways to make sure you are prepared on the golf course.

Read books on the game. (Good for you, you're already doing that!) Libraries and bookstores offer numerous titles, depending on your focus. Reading a book of USGA rules from cover to cover may sound tedious, but it will give you the specifics about the rules that govern the game (I offer some abbreviated basics in Chapter 5). You can also find books on how to lower your score, improve your swing, etc. Some golf books are timeless. For example, Ben Hogan's *Five Lessons: The Modern Fundamentals of Golf,* first published in 1957, is still in print.

Watch the Golf Channel. The Golf Channel offers many helpful tips, explains rules of the game, and shows tons of golf. You can learn a lot by watching PGA members play. Really. I tried putting with my 3-wood when I was on the fringe of the green after seeing Tiger Woods do it on the Golf Channel. And you know what? I got the ball within two inches of the hole, then sank it for par. You may learn a trick or two this way as well.

Top 10 of Golf Fashion

1. Wear a fingerless glove to show off a stylish manicure
2. Get golf shoes in every color
3. No "Daisy Duke" shorts on the course
4. Consider wearing waterproof mascara
5. Sunscreen is your friend
6. Save your bangles for the Ball
7. Remember to wear pants with pockets
8. Lose the Kentucky Derby hat
9. Choose a bra that provides ample support
10. Your best asset is your smile!

Look for helpful tips on golf-related Web sites. Although I'm suggesting this as a resource, keep in mind that the Internet can suck the time out of your day like a kid sucking the juice out of an Otter Pop. There are some great golf sites out there, but reading all the information in the world won't help your game as much as practice will.

Read *Golf for Women* magazine. There's a lot of good information packed into this magazine, plus other fun stuff just for golfing gals. It's well worth the subscription price and will look great on your coffee table!

Being prepared on the golf course is crucial to feeling good, playing well, and streamlining play. There are many ways to prepare and things to consider, but as you play more frequently, the process will become second nature. Take the time to prepare before you get to the course; you—and your companions—will be grateful you did.

MORE FUN THAN A ROOT CANAL— MOST OF THE TIME
The Basics of Play

I'm hitting the woods just great—
but having a terrible time hitting out of them.
— Harry Toscano

W OW! TWO PARS in a row. Go make it three."

"I'll try," I tell my husband, as I grab my driver and head up to the tee box. I've never hit three pars in a row, but maybe today will be my lucky day.

I tee up my ball, take my stance, and hit without a practice swing. My drive is perfect, landing in the middle of the fairway. I turn toward my husband, smile, then take a bow.

"Don't get too confident," he warns.

"Just watch, here comes my third par," I say, incredulous of my luck.

I should have known better than to start talking trash. My boasting must have irked the Par Gods, because my second shot lands in the trap.

"I can handle the beach," I say, still confident, despite my situation. "I'm from San Diego, remember? I practically grew up in the sand."

When I get to the trap, I can barely see my ball. It's a "fried egg"—almost completely covered in sand—and the trap is deep, its sides much steeper than I realized when looking from across the fairway.

"Crap," I mutter. "This sucks." I grab my wedge and dig my heels into the sand, securing my stance in the white hell. I swing and the ball doesn't move. I think about my possible par. On my next try I will have to launch the ball out of the trap and land it in the hole in order to preserve my streak. Unlikely, but possible. I say a prayer, hold my breath, and swing again. The Par Gods laugh.

This time I make contact with the ball but fail to get under it enough to clear the embankment. The ball bounces off the side of the trap and rolls like a homing pigeon back to the same spot. My par is gone. Damn.

I try again. In instant replay, my ball ricochets off the bank and lands at my feet. Now I'm pissed. My husband and the other two players in our group wait, watching me. The pressure is on. I try to clear the trap a fourth time, cursing under my breath ... and I miss. Sand flies around me like a desert storm, but when the cloud clears my ball is still in the same spot. Hope is gone. I am humiliated. I want to cry.

"Just pick it up, Honey," says my husband, his voice full of pity.

I take a 10. Who hits two pars and then a 10? Me. Often. And though I love the game of golf, sometimes playing it is more painful than a root canal.

Golf is a roller-coaster of highs and lows. When you first start, you may feel devoid of all athletic skill. Then as soon as you decide to quit and take up knitting, you'll hit a perfect shot, giving you just enough hope to keep on going. There's much to learn in the beginning; the roller-coaster can leave you nauseated and swearing like a sailor. Even when you know what to do, the shots don't always fall your way. It's part of the learning process. This chapter is designed to help you on the course. If you're just not connecting on a certain day, I've also included some tips on how to survive the round without having a mental breakdown, or just as bad, annoying the other players in your group with your whining.

CLUBS

I must admit, when I first started to play the game, I found golf clubs very confusing. I knew to use a driver off the tee and a putter on the green, but club selection on the fairway remained a mystery. How did a 7-iron differ from a 5-iron? If close to the green, did I want a high-number club, like a 9-iron, or a lower number, like a 3? I could never remember. Here's what I needed to know:

When playing golf, you are allowed 14 clubs in your bag. You may have any combination, just as long as you have no more than 14. These clubs usually consist of a driver, a putter, and some combination of woods and irons. What are woods and irons? I'm glad you asked.

Woods

A wood has a hearty club head and (generally) a longer shaft than an iron. A driver is part of the wood family and is the largest. A driver is considered a 1-wood. Other woods include numbers 3, 4, 5, 7, 9, and 11. Most players carry a driver, a 3-wood, and a 5-wood. A few players carry a 7-wood, a 9-wood, or an 11-wood. As a new golfer, I found that I hit my woods better than my irons; they had a bigger club face and therefore increased my chances of making some sort of contact. In addition, when hit correctly, woods provide more loft and distance than an iron of the same number.

Once upon a time, woods were made of wood (hence the name), but now woods are commonly made of graphite, titanium, or other metals. If you want to see an original wood, check with your grandfather; he may have one. They are also fairly common at garage sales—and if they're in good condition, they can be used for decoration (use two as a curtain rod or just hang them on the wall of your office).

Irons

Irons make up the majority of clubs in your

bag. A typical set of irons might include a 3, 4, 5, 6, 7, 8, and 9. Depending on the club, irons have a different loft angle and shaft length. Here's what always confused me: The lower the number, the flatter the club face and the longer the shaft; conversely, the higher the number, the more angled the club face and the shorter the shaft. What does this mean?

The low-number clubs, like a 3- or a 4-iron, are designed to hit the ball low and far; the high-number clubs, like an 8 or a 9, are designed to hit the ball a shorter distance and with more loft. Make sense? Think of your journey down the fairway like counting to 10. You might tee off with a driver (No. 1), then hit a 3-wood for your next shot to carry the ball as far as possible.

Depending on where you land, your next shot might be a 5- or a 7-iron, or if you're closer to the green, you might use an 8- or a 9-iron. Imagine that your pitching wedge has a 10 on it. Use it for chips up to the putting green from close range. (This example is just to illustrate club selection as you move down the fairway. On any given hole you may only use a few clubs; you must decide how far you need to hit each shot and select the appropriate club.) On a par-5 for example, I commonly tee off with my driver, then use my 3-wood a couple times to get the maximum distance possible down the fairway. As I get closer to the green, I'll select an appropriate iron or wedge to get me on the putting green.

Wedges

Wedges are irons designed to provide more loft and a shorter carry to the ball; most all wedges have a loft angle between 45 and 60 degrees. Most players carry a pitching wedge and a sand wedge in their bag. A typical sand wedge has a 54- to 57-degree angle, and a pitching wedge usually falls between 45 and 49 degrees. Other wedges available are a gap wedge and a lob wedge. A gap wedge, also called an attack wedge or a dual wedge, falls between a sand wedge and pitching wedge and typically has a 49- to 54-degree loft angle. A lob wedge is 57 degrees or more. (You might also have heard of a "foot wedge." This is what I needed in my sand trap fiasco. It always works, but of course it's not technically permitted in the rules of golf.)

The greater the angle, the more loft a club will provide. For example, a sand wedge is a very angled club. It's designed so one can (theoretically) pop the ball out of a bunker with relative ease. As noted by my experience, it doesn't always work that way. However, it's wise to practice with your wedges. In *Break 100 Now!* Mike Adams and T. J. Tomasi note that "70% of shots are within 100 yards of the green." This means mastery of your short game (wedges and putter) is crucial. Adams and Tomasi also advise newer golfers to carry a 60-degree wedge (lob wedge), so they can still swing fully on a short approach. This is good advice, as I had poor consistency with a half swing when I was learning and would frequently launch my ball from one side of the green to the other. Ugh!

CLUB SELECTION

As a new golfer, you may not want or be able to invest tons of money in clubs. Do your best to find clubs that are a good fit for you in shaft length, grip, and assortment. If you're serious about the game and have the funds, seek the advice of a qualified professional when purchasing clubs. Ask to try out clubs to get a feel for what works best for you. Clubs are a big investment and can make or break your game. Choose wisely.

If you're clueless about what to put in your bag, here are a few thoughts to keep in mind. As I mentioned, when I first started I couldn't hit my irons very well. The lower irons are especially hard to hit, so I'd suggest taking them out of your bag and adding additional woods. Adams and Tomasi make the point that woods are "easier to hit than long irons from any lie—from the rough, from a divot, off the tee. They also produce shots that fly higher and straighter (because they give more loft, which creates more backspin and less sidespin) and land softer, making it easier to keep your ball on the green on approach shots." For this reason, the authors suggest removing the 3-iron from your bag completely and using a 7-wood in place of a 4-iron.

I did this and it helped my game. In my bag I carry a driver, 3-wood, 5-wood, 7-wood, irons 5 through 9, a sand wedge, pitching wedge and putter. This is a total of 12 clubs. I'm allowed 14, so if I want to add a lob wedge or a 9-wood, I can. These 12 work for me and keep my bag a little lighter for when I carry my clubs on the course. If you always use a cart and want the extra clubs, then by all means bring them. Again, try some clubs, decide what you like, and organize your bag based on what works best for *you*.

Note: Some irons are now available in a fairway wood/iron hybrid. These clubs play like traditional irons but have a bit more chunk to them, like a wood, providing the benefits of both. My 5- and 6-iron are hybrids, and I love them.

BAG ORGANIZATION

Keeping your bag organized is crucial to keeping track of your clubs and quick club selection. I'll admit, it makes sense to do this, but it took me a long time to actually keep my bag organized. Now that I stick to a system, I'm more efficient and can inventory at a glance, making sure I haven't left a club somewhere. (This is important, especially if you've just spent the bank on new clubs!)

Most bags have four main sections for club storage. For ease, I group my clubs by type. At the top of my bag, or in the biggest section, I keep my driver and woods with head covers to keep them from clanking together. I keep my Nos. 5 and 6 hybrid irons in another section, I group my 7-, 8-, and 9-irons and my wedges and putter together. This works for me. Some experts might suggest a different grouping, but decide what logically works for you and stick to it. Nobody will be playing with your clubs except you.

THE NITTY GRITTY OF PLAY

I'm just going to run through the basics here. Remember, this is not a comprehensive guide and these tips do not replace lessons. They are basic pointers that I've found helpful to my game. I think they'll help you too.

Teeing off

You can only tee up your ball when you hit off the tee box. Place your tee between the round red tee-box markers and either level with or up to two club lengths behind them. You cannot place your ball forward of the tee-box markers when you tee off.

Whoever won the last hole has the "honor,"

or tees off first on the next hole. For example, if Carolyn shoots par on hole No. 5 and I make a bogey, then she would have the honor of teeing off first on No. 6.

If we tie, whoever teed up first keeps the honor on the next hole. For example, if Carolyn and I both score birdies on the sixth hole, she would tee off first again on No. 7, because she still has the honor from winning hole No. 5.

Watch where your ball goes when you hit. Identify landmarks around where it lands, such as a listing pine tree or a large bush, so you can locate it quickly.

Follow the direction of your partner's ball as well. Generally, when I play with girls, I can keep track of their balls because they don't tend to fly beyond my sight range. But when I play with my husband, I often lose track of his ball—especially when it disappears against the backdrop of cloud cover. You won't see where every ball lands—just try your best to be attentive.

On the fairway
If you're having trouble controlling your ball, try choking down on the club.

If the wind is blowing like crazy, pull your hair back to keep it out of your eyes and adjust your stance when you hit. For example, if there is a strong right-to-left wind, aim your ball more to the right to compensate.

Watch for yardage markers that indicate your distance from the green. Then make an educated club selection based on how far you can hit each club.

Be sure you can identify your ball, and do not hit someone else's. You might initial yours with a permanent marker if you have trouble remembering.

Repair divots you make in the fairway. If you hit a chunk of grass out of the ground, retrieve the clump, replace it, and step on it to smooth it back down. If it breaks into a zillion small pieces, fill the spot by pouring some sand mixture on the area. (This is usually provided in the cart).

Sand and water ... ugh!

Avoid hitting toward hazards such as sand and water. Most courses provide a scorecard with an outline of each hole. Review them. Some carts also have electronic monitors that tell you the distance (from the green) and location of water hazards—pay attention and orient yourself with this information. If you need to drive the cart up and look over a hill to locate the bunkers, do it. (Make sure no one is hitting before you zip up the fairway!) I cannot tell you how many times I've forgotten to aim because I was so focused on the ball. You can land a great shot in the bunker if you don't plan ahead.

When you hit into a sand trap, enter the trap at the point closest to your ball. Do not touch the sand with your club before you hit or you will incur a penalty stroke. Rake the trap after you hit.

If your sand trap experiences are like mine—an irritating *Groundhog Day*-like repetition of the same crappy shot—keep these tips in mind:

If you need to hit a long distance out of the trap, try to "pick it clean." This means hitting the ball without touching the sand. If you need to pop the ball up and onto the green a short distance away, hit behind the ball, into the sand. Often, flying the green or beaming a ball out of the sand trap has less to do with how hard you hit the ball than where you hit the sand behind it.

For loft, play the ball off your front foot with an open club face.

Pay attention

Keep an accurate count of your score. When I first started, I'd always tell my husband, "I think I had an eight" or ask him, "How many shots did I take on that hole?" Not good. Your partner is not responsible for your score, you are. If you hit so many shots that you lose count (as in my case), then invest in a small counter. You can attach it to your belt and click it every time you hit the ball.

When you're playing with others, the one whose ball is farthest from the pin hits first. Then the next person farthest out would hit, and so on.

"Ready golf" is hitting when you are ready (and not necessarily in proper sequence) in order to speed up play. Make sure all players agree in advance if you're going to play ready golf so nobody gets frustrated because they think you're breaking protocol by hitting before them.

The putting green

Keep all golf carts, push carts, and golf bags off the putting green.

Just like on the fairway, whoever is farthest from the pin goes first.

Always mark your ball. Do this by placing a marker behind your ball, then picking up your ball. When it's your turn to putt, replace your ball and then pick up the marker. Note: In a friendly game, you may only need to mark a ball if it's in line with another player's putt to the hole.

Be careful not to walk across someone's putting line (the imaginary line from the ball to the hole). Also be sure your shadow does not fall across their line or the hole, hindering their view.

Go to your ball and plan your putt while others take their turn—do not disturb them!

Assess the "break" of the green and determine which way your ball will roll. Putt accordingly.

If you hit your ball close enough to the hole to guarantee an easy tap-in, other players may say, "I'll give you that" or "That's a gimme." You must count your gimmes. I learned this the hard way.

On one par-4, I reached the green in three and putted my fourth shot within an inch of the cup.

"That's a gimme," said my husband.

"I got a par!" I exclaimed, beaming. I grabbed my ball and excitedly jumped up and down.

"How do you figure?" he asked, a smirk on his face.

"Well, if you are *giving it to me*, then I only took four strokes," I said. My husband threw back his head and let out a hearty guffaw.

"You have to count your gimmes," he said, shaking his head at my naïveté. "OK, well, I guess I get a bogey then," I said, feeling like a deflated party balloon.

So count your gimmes. (And when they are offered to you, take them; you never know when you might miss a gimme putt and end up with even more strokes on your scorecard.)

After you hit your ball into the hole, pick it up. Some players are superstitious and do not like to hit their ball into the hole while another ball is in there.

When you move on to the next hole, check the green for clubs that you might be leaving behind and replace the flagstick for the next group.

Pace of play

Make sure to keep up the pace of play by focusing on the game and making sure you're prepared.

Don't spend too much time looking for a wayward ball. If you hit into long grass and see where the ball goes in, stomping your feet around the area is a good technique for finding your ball. Poking a club around won't be as effective and you don't want to reach with your hand—you might find a snake! Just stomp those feet, girls!

If you are new and playing a friendly game with experienced golfers, don't feel like you must play every shot. When you're learning, it's OK to hit, retrieve your ball, and then take a drop near the ball of a better player for your next hit. This helps keep up the pace of play (and can help reduce frustration).

Likewise, if you're a new golfer and are already at double par, consider picking up your ball until you reach the green. (As long as you're not playing in a tournament or some sort of competition, who cares? You're learning.) There is no point in frustrating yourself, irritating your partners, or slowing the game.

If you're playing slowly and a faster group is behind you, consider letting them play through.

Drive your cart forward to the next tee box before recording your scores and cleaning your clubs. This will also help keep up the pace of play.

FOOD

If the beverage and snack cart comes around when you're across the fairway taking a shot, ask if a friend will grab you something or finish your shot and then run over to the snack cart. Move quickly to avoid delaying the game.

Take care that chip bags and candy bar wrappers do not blow out of your golf cart, leaving litter on the fairway. Deposit trash in the trashcans around the course (usually located at the start of each hole).

Eat snacks regularly and stay hydrated. I have skipped breakfast for early morning golf and later felt dizzy. Bad. Bad. Bad. Take care of your body, and it will help your game.

Speaking of help ... if you are PMSing about your game, frustrated, and ready to quit, have a "cool one." Sometimes a cool drink will help relax you just enough to take the edge off and get you back to enjoying the game.

THE LADIES ROOM

When you go to the bathroom, remember to take off your golf glove! Once, when I was in a big rush to get back to the game, I ran in, sat down to pee, and then realized I had not taken off my glove. Yuck! You're never in *that* much of a hurry!

If the cart key is needed to unlock the restroom, remember to bring the key back out with you. These mid-course bathroom doors often lock automatically, and if you rush back to your game leaving the cart key behind, you're going to have a problem.

When using a Port-a-Potty, be careful not to drop your sunglasses (or cell phone) into the pit!

FOCUS ON THE EXPERIENCE

Frustration, embarrassment, and being otherwise agitated will not help your game. If you shank a shot, take a deep breath and get some perspective. It's more fun to play with someone new to the game who follows protocol and has a cheerful attitude than it is to play with a more experienced golfer who throws a tantrum with every errant shot.

> ## Top 10 Things Consumed on a Golf Course
>
> 1. Hot dog
> 2. Sports drink
> 3. Candy bar
> 4. Turkey sandwich
> 5. Breakfast burrito
> 6. Water
> 7. Soda
> 8. Beer
> 9. Beer
> 10. Beer

Don't try to be competitive when you're new to the sport. Just enjoy the opportunity to play and learn.

Laugh when you feel like crying.

When the round is over, shake your partner's hand (or kiss your hubby, if you're playing with him).

Be thankful for the opportunity to play. Remember, you could be home working on an

Excel chart for a sales presentation, grocery shopping, or changing a diaper. Golf is a break from the routine. It is exercise, fresh air, fellowship—and a chance to challenge yourself. Gobble it up.

FRIED EGGS AND THE DANCE FLOOR
Terminology Clarified

I don't say my golf game is bad,
but if I grew tomatoes, they'd come up sliced.

— Anonymous

Y OU HIT THAT kind of thin, Honey. I think you might be in the bunker."

"That sucks," I say, wondering what "hitting it thin" means.

"Yep, you're in the beach," he says as we drive the cart over to the sand trap. "And look at that fried egg!"

"I don't even see my ball," I say, "And what's a fried egg?"

"*That* is a fried egg," he tells me, motioning to a small white spot in the corner of the bunker. I walk over and peer down. My ball is buried in the sand, with only a bit of the top exposed.

After several profanities, I escape the hazard and prepare for my next shot.

"The course is a dogleg left right there," yells my husband as he grabs clubs and heads toward his ball. "Try to hook it."

"A dog is on the course where?" I ask, confused, my eyes scanning the area for a wayward animal. Distracted, my next shot is a fast-moving scuttle ball—it skims the ground like a misdirected missile flying only inches from the earth.

"That's a worm burner if I ever saw one!" says my friend waiting in the cart behind me.

"A what?" I ask, getting more confused with each shot. What is a *worm burner*?

Our foursome nears the hole. My husband chips his ball up toward the green.

"Bite! Bite!" he yells, as he watches his ball fly through the air.

"You're OK," says one friend. "I think you're on the dance floor."

"I think you might be in the frog hair," comments the other.

"What are you all talking about?" I ask, straining to see where my husband's ball has gone. Bite? Frog hair? Was I playing golf, or had I been kidnapped by a band of double-talkers? Before the round is over I hear a dozen more terms that challenge my current knowledge of links lingo. This isn't *Jeopardy*; this is golf. Yet, I feel as clueless as Gilligan, always asking for clarification of what seems to be common knowledge to everyone except me.

Golf terminology can be confusing. If you're a new player trying to decipher the meaning of certain phraseology, it is distracting and downright irritating. Here, listed by category, are all the terms I have encountered on the course. Some of them you may already know; some you never may have heard. Either way, learn them. Imagine you are in sixth grade and need to memorize vocabulary for a test.

Knowing the terms won't necessarily get you an "A" in golf, but it will help your game and improve your enjoyment of each round. You probably won't impress anyone, but being "in the know" is much better than feeling like a golf outsider—lost somewhere in the gunch.

BASIC ACRONYMS

USGA: United States Golf Association

PGA: Professional Golf Association

LPGA: Ladies Professional Golf Association

NCGA: Novice, Clueless Golf Amateurs (a term I coined myself)

EQUIPMENT AND PLACES

Golf ball: OK, I started easy. This is the little white ball you hit. It's covered with dimples, not unlike the dimples on my cheeks—that is, the cheeks on my face—multiplied.

Clubs: The collection of irons, woods, and putter that you use to hit the ball. (Depending on your score, you may feel the urge to smack a tree or slam them into the ground. Restrain yourself; you'll regret it later if you lose your cool.)

Irons: Irons make up the majority of clubs in your bag, usually numbers 3 to 9. (They bear no relation to the other irons in your life: curling iron, flatiron, steam iron, though using an iron on the fairway and ironing a pile of shirts can sometimes produce the same sense of hopelessness and despair—or pressing accomplishment!)

Woods: A wood has a longer shaft and a bigger club face than an iron. These clubs typically give you more loft and distance than an iron. (Woods are not named after Tiger Woods, though one might think so! Actually, these clubs were once made of wood, and the name stuck.)

Wedge: A shorter iron with a more angled club face. It is designed to hit the ball a shorter distance and give it more loft. (It can also be an uncomfortable gathering of underwear requiring discreet readjustment).

Sand wedge: Primarily used to escape the bunker. The club face is typically angled 54 to 57 degrees and provides lots of loft to pop the ball up-up-up!

Pitching wedge: Mostly used when short of the green to "pitch" onto the putting surface. These clubs typically are angled between 45 and 49 degrees.

Gap wedge: Falls between a sand wedge and a pitching wedge. It can also be referred to as a "dual" or "attack" wedge.

Lob wedge: A great club for newer players. This wedge has 57 or more degrees of angle for lots of loft and a short carry.

Foot wedge: Love this! The foot wedge never fails, but unfortunately, it's illegal. No, the police won't arrest you, but it is against the rules of the game. (It is using your foot to kick the ball out of the trap, a technique typically employed to prevent a mental breakdown.)

Driver: The 1-wood, primarily used to hit off the tee box. (It is *not* the gentleman who drove the limo to the prom!)

Putter: The flat-faced club you use on the green to putt the ball into the cup.

Head covers: The common term for the little pouches that protect your woods and driver. They may be plain, resemble fury stuffed animals, or bear the logo of your college alma mater. My favorite head cover is a chicken that holds an extra golf ball in her backside. So funny!

(Note: Girls tend to like the animal-type head covers, and I think they give a little personality to your clubs. Just one word of caution: Be careful to either replace head covers after you hit or secure them in your cart basket, otherwise you may lose that ol' chicken and her egg along the fairway as you zip along in the cart.)

Pull cart: A handy-dandy cart you can pull behind you (or push in front of you) that holds your clubs when you walk the course.

Carry bag: A lightweight bag with legs that prop it up when you set it down. Carry bags usually come with shoulder straps for when you walk the course—and carry your clubs. (Good exercise!)

Cart bag: A golf bag designed to be used primarily with some type of cart (a golf cart or a pull cart). I once tried to walk nine holes with a friend, not realizing that my bag was a cart bag. It was uncomfortable on my shoulders and kept falling over when I set it down—very annoying to me and other players. I felt like a player from the 1920s, laying my bag down flat each time I took a shot. It was time-consuming and difficult to dig clubs from the bag. Plus, I looked ridiculous. If you plan on walking at all, invest in a carry bag. (You can put a carry bag on a cart, but carrying a cart bag is more difficult.)

Golf cart: The zippy (or pathetically slow) vehicle in which you ride on the course. Most carts are an additional charge to greens fees, but if you are playing 18 holes and want to keep up pace of play, it's not a bad idea. A golf cart means less exercise but more convenience. Some are electric and quiet—others can be *loud*, like a John Deere tractor.

Cart path: The little road designed for golf carts that winds through the course. The cart path is to you what the yellow brick road was to Dorothy; follow it and it will lead you where you want to go.

Clubhouse: The main building at a golf course. Usually the pro shop, restrooms, and a restaurant and/or snack bar are located in the clubhouse.

Pro shop: Usually located in the clubhouse, this is where you make tee-time reservations, pay for your round, shop for golf merchandise, purchase extra balls, etc. The staff in the pro shop also usually can answer any questions you might have about the course.

Driving range: An area with distance markers, clubs, balls, and tees where you can practice hitting the ball. You'll want to visit the driving range as often as possible—haunt it like your favorite bar in college. Go a couple times a week, if possible. Practice before a round of play, and hit balls after work. The more you practice, the better you'll be.

The 19th hole: The post-round hotspot where you can relax and review your game over a round of drinks. It's the bar.

ON THE COURSE, OF COURSE!

Tee box: The marked location where you start play on each hole. Players of different skill levels or gender may hit from different tee boxes. Women primarily hit from the red tees.

Red tees: The tee-box start for women—appropriately named because the "red" color generally matches the color of your cheeks when you whiff a shot. (Though the women's tees are *usually* red, they can be other colors, so check to make sure you're hitting from the correct location.)

Caddie: The person who carries and cleans your clubs and ball and helps you with just about everything except hitting the ball. (Darn. That's what I usually need help with most!) A good caddie is like having a personal assistant on the course.

Mulligan: A repeat shot off the tee box. Mulligans are not regulation, but they are commonly taken in a friendly game.

Fairway: The manicured green area between the tee box and the putting green.

Green: The pristine area of the course where you putt your ball. It's also known as the putting green or the dance floor. (A new player can also be "green," as in naïve and unskilled.)

Dogleg: A bend in the geography of the course. Imagine the shape of Fido's back haunches, and apply that to the fairway. You've got it.

Water: The beverage you need to drink a lot of during play, and also what you want to avoid on the course when hitting your ball.

Hazard: A pond, lake, or any other body of water you want to avoid on the fairway is a water hazard. A sand bunker is a hazard. Visible panty lines are a hazard. Avoid at all costs!

Bunker: A sand or grass trap is a bunker. This can also refer to an out-of-town friend who stays at your house for a golf weekend.

Gunch: The long, unmanicured grass surrounding the fairway. The gunch can also be out-of-bounds. You want to avoid the gunch. Think of it as a ball eater, time stealer, and score destroyer. (The gunch is not to be confused with the Grinch, who is an onion eater, gift stealer, and Christmas destroyer.)

Beach: The nontechnical term for the bunker. The sand ... the beach ... you get it. If you're on a tropical golf vacation, the beach is where you relax after an invigorating round on the links.

Dance floor: A term commonly used to describe the putting green. It's also my favorite place at a wedding (aside from the cake line).

SCORE-RELATED LINGO

Score: The total of all your hits per round. A score is a relative term—some courses are harder than others, and we all have bad days. Don't let a bad score ruin your day; do let a good score give you a cheerful boost.

Scorecard: The small card on which you record your hits per hole. The scorecard also has valuable information on course rules, slope, rating, par, and handicap holes. (After a subpar round you may want to destroy your scorecard; after a superb round, you may want to post it on the events board at the clubhouse.)

Penalty: The strokes you add to your score for breaking a rule. (The number varies depending on the offense.)

Par: The average number of shots a player should take from the tee to sinking the putt on the green. (I think it should stand for **P**ersistently **A**ggravating **R**eality.)

Birdie: Scoring one stroke less than par. Very good! (A birdie can also be the feathered creature that poops on your head the one day you decide not to wear a hat.)

Eagle: Scoring two strokes under par. *Wahoo!* (Like a birdie, an eagle can also poop on your head.)

Bogey: Shooting one stroke over par. Example: If par is four shots and you've taken five, you've scored a bogey. Something to remember: Scoring a bogey on all 18 holes would total 90 strokes—not too bad!

Double bogey: Two strokes over par on a hole.

Triple bogey: Three strokes over par. Ouch! This just sucks.

Ace: The term for a hole-in-one. Yeah! (Your babysitter may also be your "ace." You gotta love someone who plays with your kids while you play, too.)

Handicap: The difficulty rating of a particular hole on a course. It's also a term to describe how many shots you average over par. For example, if you are a "zero handicap," you are a "scratch golfer." If your handicap is an 8, then you usually shoot an 80 (eight over par).

GHIN number: Acronym for "Golfers Handicap Information Network." This is a number you can acquire and enter your scores under (in a course computer or on line) which refers to your handicap. Your GHIN number is pronounced "Gin," like the drink.

Slope/rating: The length and difficulty rating of a particular course. The slope and rating are usually listed on the scorecard, unless you are playing a par-3 or executive course, which generally do not have a slope and difficulty rating.

GOLF-SPEAK

Hacker: The nontechnical term for a nontechnical golfer. When you first start to play, you are a hacker. You'll soon discover why this term fits.

Duffer: An average, everyday golfer.

Scratch golfer: A golfer who, on average, shoots par every round. (If you know any scratch golfers, listen to them. Watch them. Learn from them. Become to them what peanut butter is to jelly—inseparable; it may help your game!)

"Pro": A qualified instructor who teaches the game of golf and/or has played the sport competitively.

Choke down: Moving your hands down the shaft of a long club to gain more control. Even if you choke down, you may still choke.

Choke: To screw up a shot. (You can also choke if you bite off too much hot dog when going over a bump while driving the cart.)

Crush: To hit the bejeebers out of the ball. To hit a great, long shot. Generally, if you hear, "Geez, you crushed that," it's a good thing.

Shank: To hit a shot poorly, often making contact with the hosel—the neck of the iron club head. A shank usually flies at a right angle to where you actually wanted the ball to go. This is not so good. (Unfortunately, I am very familiar with this term.)

Provisional ball: A ball you hit if you happen to "crush" or "shank" your original ball and cannot find it. You must take a penalty stroke if you lose your original ball and continue to play the provisional. (If you do this, the provisional is no longer a "provisional," but the active ball in play.)

Whiff: To swing and miss the ball completely. (Argh!) The difference between a whiff and a practice swing is your intent; if you meant to hit the ball, it's a whiff and you count the stroke.

Bite: Although this could be a good chomp on your 10th-hole Snickers, it generally means for the ball to stop. When someone yells, "Bite! Bite!" they want their ball to slow down and stop. Another less common definition refers to what the summer mosquitoes can do to your legs. If you live or play in a buggy area, I suggest using a sunscreen with insect repellent to keep pests away. Generally, your game can eat you alive; you don't need bugs to do it, too.

Hook: The flight of a ball that deviates from a straight line in the direction opposite from the player's dominant hand. (If you're right-handed and hook the ball, it curves to the left; if you're a lefty, the ball curves right.) You can hook the ball on purpose (skilled golfer) or accidentally (hacker).

Draw: Similar to a hook, except that (for right-handed golfers) the ball initially flies straight right of the fairway, then slowly bends inward to the left. (For lefties, the ball would sail straight left of the fairway before bending to the right. (Draw is also what you can do on the scorecard with the itty-bitty golf pencil after giving up play. No! Never quit!)

Kick: A bounce of the ball. If your ball hits the cart path and bounces onto the fairway, it is said to "kick" onto the fairway. (This is also what you might find yourself doing to the golf cart after you whiff a ball for the third time in a row.)

Slice: When the ball has outside rotating spin causing it to go to the right, for right-handers. (It's the opposite if you're hitting left.)

Fade: The opposite of a draw, but not as severe. The ball drifts to the outside while in the air. (Your smile may also "fade" if you are not hitting the ball as well as you'd like.)

Cut: A slice.

Spin: What your head is doing with information overload. Take a deep breath. Now exhale. *Ahhhhh.* OK, let's press on.

Chip: A short-game shot, often hit with a wedge. You "chip" the ball up onto the green when you hit a short-distance shot.

Pitch: Also a short-game shot. The ball flies high and lands soft.

Hit: What you want to do to the ball. My motto is this: Contact is good!

Open club face: The position of your club when the face is tilted toward the sky. Theoretically, the more "open" your club face when you hit, the more loft on the ball.

Closed club face: The position of your club when the face is tilted down over the ball.

Hitting fat: Hitting too far under the ball. If you "hit fat," you may get mud on your club.

Hitting thin: Not getting completely under the ball when you hit it. If you catch the edge of your club on the ball, you are "hitting thin."

Backspin: Backward rotation on the ball after you hit it. Great players can put backspin on a ball; most cannot.

Divot: A chunk of grass that comes up with your club when you hit the ball. If possible, repair divot holes by reinserting the clump of grass and pressing it down with your foot, or by filling the hole with a repair mixture provided by the course. (This is usually supplied in the cart.)

Putt: Hitting your ball while on the green in an attempt to get it into the ever-elusive hole.

Gimme: A stroke (in putting) that you don't have to take because the ball is so close to the hole it would be almost impossible to miss. Though other players may grant you a gimme, you still have to count the stroke.

Speed control: Necessary for good, consistent putting. It's harder than it sounds.

Break: The way the ball will roll on the green, depending on the slope of the surface. (It's also something you'll wish you had after about 13 holes—especially if you're a new player.)

Hole out: Hitting the ball into the hole in one shot, or to finish putting.

"Fore!": What you yell when your wayward ball is headed toward a person or a group of people. This expression warns everyone of the impending danger, letting them cover their heads or look up to see where the ball is—only to get hit directly in the face by it. If your ball looks like it might be on course to hit someone, break out your inner cheerleader and holler "FORE!" as loudly as you can—don't be shy. It could save someone's life.

Stroke play: The term used when players compete swing for swing. Most games are stroke play, and the player taking the fewest strokes wins.

Match play: When players compete hole by hole. For example, if you win the first two holes and your partner wins the third, you are up one hole with 15 remaining. In match play, whoever wins the most holes is the champion.

Press: Starting a new bet. The team that presses is usually losing—so when a friendly wager wanes, this keeps things interesting. For example, if you are down three holes, you might "press" and hope to beat your opponents on the next bet.

Skins play: Essentially, a competition for each individual hole. Tied holes carry over to the next hole, and if two people tie, then everyone ties. For example, let's say I play in a game of skins with my husband and three of his friends, and we decide each hole is worth $5, or a "skin," to the winning player. For the first four holes, the two best players tie, so we all tie, and the value of each hole carries over to the next.

On the fifth hole, if I (technically the worst golfer) have a great hole and shoot par and everyone else bogeys, then I win $25—$5 for the hole and $5 each for the four previous holes. Even if you're not a great golfer, you can do well at skins if you get lucky and win a couple of holes. If you're playing with your husband and have a new baby at home, make it interesting. Make each skin worth a diaper change! (You probably change the most anyway, so you have nothing to lose and everything to gain!)

Tournament: An event in which a group of golfers plays competitively. Your local golf club might have a "club tournament," in which all the members compete in stroke play, or a charity tournament that is a team scramble. Rules and guidelines will vary from tournament to tournament, so make sure you know the rules prior to playing.

Sandbagger: Someone who artificially inflates his or her handicap in order to win tournaments. A sandbagger is a disgrace to the golfing community.

Flight: A grouping of players, often used in league play.

Shotgun start: A format, generally used in tournament and sometimes league play, in which all players (or teams) start on different holes at the same time. For example, everyone would be assigned a specific hole on which to begin play and would drive to that hole—then at the shotgun start, the groups at each hole would begin play at the same time. If, in a shotgun start, you begin play on hole No. 7, you'll finish on hole No. 6. Make sure to mark your scorecard according to the hole you start on (in this case, begin with No. 7, not No. 1; otherwise you'll have a big mess).

League: A group of golfers, through a club or community center, that plays rounds together on a regular basis. Many leagues are competitive; others are more relaxed and just for fun.

Scramble: A playing format in which everyone in a group hits, then the best shot is selected and everyone hits from that spot. You pick the best ball from the next round of hits, everyone plays from there, and so on. Scrambles are often used in charity golf tournaments. (Contrary to popular belief, scramble is *not* what you did to your eggs this morning.)

SAY WHAT?!

Victory lap: The dramatic little circle your ball makes around the edge of the cup before dropping into the hole. (It's also what you take on the golf course after sinking a hole-in-one. Just kidding.)

"Liprish": Similar to a victory lap, but instead of the ball dropping into the hole, it rolls on the lip of the cup but slips off the edge and travels back onto the green. If you catch the lip of a hole more than twice on one hole, you may have a nasty case of "liprish."

Frog hair: You didn't know frogs had hair? Neither did I. Frog hair is the grassy area just short of the putting green.

Leaving chicken on the bone: When your putt stops just a little short of the hole but is too far away to be a gimme. Bummer.

Sh** on your stick: Mud that clings to the bottom of your club when you catch the ground and hit the ball fat. It's more of a joke than an actual golfing term, but I'm telling you so you don't fall for it. Once when I was hitting on the fairway, I caught the ground and ended up with a big chunk of mud on the end of my iron. My oh-so-charming husband said, "Celeste, you have a little sh** on the end of your stick." I looked at the muddy end of my club. "No, the other end," he said, laughing. Very funny.

Chili-dip: Hitting the ground before you hit the ball, causing it not to go very far. This is no Super Bowl dish; it's a bad shot that may plague a new player's game, and it may also render a little "sh** on your stick." (Chili-dips are more common in my short game. When I try to just chip up to the green, without beaming the ball too far, I sometimes tend to hit down, resulting in an old-fashioned chili-dip.)

Fried egg: A ball buried in a sand bunker with only its top half exposed. So named because it looks a lot like something you might eat for breakfast.

Worm burner: A ball that skims the ground—supposedly "burning" the worms that might pop up out of the ground as that earth-loving ball blasts past.

Husband golf: Taking advice, solicited or not, from your husband/boyfriend/golf partner. While it may be helpful at times, it's generally a recipe for disaster. Play your own game.

Snowman: A common term for an eight (8) on your scorecard.

Cart tart: The lesser-known name for the sexy girl who drives the beverage cart. (If she's a hottie and your boyfriend is suddenly parched, beware.)

Bag boy: The chap who cleans your clubs when you finish a round and takes them to your car. Tip these guys—many people don't, and it's hot out there!

Shagging balls: Although this sounds like a kinky Austin Powers pastime, it's the term used to describe what the attendant does when he picks up the balls on the driving range.

FRUSTRATION-RELATED MUMBLINGS

Damn: A borderline profanity you may mutter under your breath (or shout at the top of your lungs) if you miss a putt by an inch or less.

Crap: Another term you may yell when frustrated on the golf course, or what you may see around the edge of a duck pond on the course.

#$!!*@&%!: Any number of profanities that might inadvertently escape your beautifully glossed lips when frustration manifests. Try to refrain; it is unbecoming—and it won't help your game.

Bitch: The nontechnical term for the girl (formerly your friend) who just beat you by five strokes. Actually, this is what you do for an hour after your round if you're not happy with how you played.

Excuses: A collection of reasons for why

you didn't play so well on a particular hole or round. From PMS to wind to low blood sugar, we all use them. How else could we justify a 116? It *couldn't be* lack of skill.

Sore loser: What you are after losing a round to a friend and then waking up the next day with back pain. You might also be called a sore loser if you "bitch" and make excuses after a round of golf. No one wants to be a sore loser—either way—so, stretch out before your round, do your best, and keep perspective if you have a bad day. It's more fun for everyone that way.

Baby: Another term for a sore loser or someone with a bad attitude. A baby is also something you should *never* have on the golf course. Don't bring along any little people to ride in the cart while you play; get a babysitter (see Chapter 8).

Babysitter: The wonderful person who agrees to watch your children while you escape for the day on the golf course. Plan ahead for your sitters—and pay them well. You want her to come back next time you go to play golf or have a night out on the town. If you're acting like a baby (immature and pouty) over a bad shot, this term might also be used to describe your golf partner for the day. No one wants to babysit you, so keep your head up and smile.

SAY IT AGAIN!

"Good ball": Words you want to hear any time you make a fabulous shot.

"Nice shot": Words of praise used to describe a spectacular hit. (If you are offering such praise, make sure the shot is actually a good one before you speak. I once told my father-in-law, "Nice shot," only to watch it then drop into the water and have him look at me like I was a complete idiot.)

MISCELLANEOUS

Sunscreen: Sunscreen good, wrinkles bad. If you're going to be in the sun, protect yourself. I know you know, but remember to reapply sunscreen during the day if needed. You don't want the red tees to match your face *and* the rest of your body.

Washrooms: Also known as a restroom or a bathroom, it's where you can go to pee, touch up your makeup, or have a good post-round cry. (Actually, don't cry in the restroom; some-one might think you're mental. If you *are* mental and need a post-round cry, then go home.)

Farmer blow: Blowing your nose forcefully (without a tissue) onto the ground. A farmer blow is often followed by a "toddler swipe," wiping the remaining snot onto a hand or shirt. Any self-respecting girl will find a washroom to blow her nose. Many males have used the FB option at one time or another.

Course guide: The person who accompa-nies you on a round, informing you of where hazards are and how to play each hole. When my husband and I got married, we played golf in Jamaica on our honeymoon and the course we played required a course guide. He was a fun old guy and helped our game. These days, you don't see many course guides out there— they've been replaced by computerized cart monitors—but if you ever have a course guide on a round, tip him. (I know watching me hit must've been a *long* day's work for our Jamaican friend!)

Shoulder season: Essentially the off-sea-son in golf. If you live in a golfing mecca, like Southern California or Arizona, there is never

Rungs on the Ladder to Par

1. Have fun
2. Be flexible
3. Take lessons
4. Learn the lingo
5. Practice
6. Make the necessary sacrifice
7. Be committed
8. Practice some more

a shoulder season. In Colorado, it can be the snowy season, where golfable days are hit and miss.

Performance anxiety: A condition, found in the bedroom and on the golf course, in which the fear of doing something wrong renders you unable to do it at all. Just relax ... at least you have your clothes on when you're on the golf course!

Stress: Constraining forces or influences that cause mental or bodily tension. Too much stress can cripple anything. Remember, golf is just a game. RELAX!

Hope: The feeling of inspiration and anticipation typical at the start of your golf day.

Good humor: The ability to laugh at yourself no matter what the day may bring. (It's also the brand of ice cream bars you can soothe your sorrows with after a bad round, should you fail to have any other "good humor.")

Prayer: The short conversation you have with God before every hit (in which you promise to volunteer at a convalescent home for the rest of your life if you can just make a hole-in-one).

Lightning: Bad news on the golf course. If you see lightning, head in and ask for a rain check. Lightning and golf do not mix!

Death: Something you may encounter if you fail to heed the advice about lightning and are zapped on the course. (A hundred fifty bucks for the round wasted—now that's a real bummer.) I joke, but this is serious stuff. Be wary of potential dangers on the course. No round is worth your life.

Hopefully, being "in the know" about golf terminology will help you feel more comfortable on the course and give you insight into the lingo of longtime players. And as you play the game, you might even develop some fun terminology of your own. Either way, you won't have to scramble off the course feeling like a sore loser because your partner just said you left some "chicken on the bone" and you didn't know what she was talking about. Just smile. Knowledge is power—even (and especially) on the golf course.

SOMETIMES
IT HURTS
Basic Rules and Scoring

Golf appeals to the idiot in us and the child.
Just how childlike golfers become is proven by their
frequent inability to count past five.

— John Updike

THE GROUP HAD been on our tail for the last several holes. We stayed far enough ahead so we didn't hinder their pace of play, yet they were always on the fairway as we finished our putts. It stressed me out. When we started the round, no one was near us, so why had a group closed in?

The foursome behind us looked to be a Saturday outing of the Boys Club, but our foursome included a girl: me. Was I the reason they were dogging our heels? Was I the guilty party? My scores were higher than the others in my group. Worried rationalizations spun through my head like those neon billboards flashing messages in Times Square: A higher score means more hits, which equals more time. As the tag-along female, was I hindering the speed of my group? I cringed under the pressure of being the stereotypical "slow female golfer."

What I failed to calculate was this: We were not behind the pace of play; according to the monitor on our cart, we were ahead of pace. The guys in my group had taken a few minutes to grab drinks while I waited for *them*, and if we had been holding up the other group, we would have waved them through. I hadn't focused on these factors, which proved my worrying unwarranted, and I wasn't focusing on something else: my game.

As we stood on the green putting out the 16th hole, I glanced over my shoulder, watching the group behind us inch closer. I wasn't planning my putt; I was worried about when we were going to clear the green and move on to the next hole.

"Celeste, it's your turn."

"Oh," I said, snapping back to take my turn for a simple two-foot putt. I hit the ball quickly, not taking time to concentrate on my shot, and the errant ball rolled way past the cup. I hit again, this time putting back toward the hole, and then tapped the third putt in.

As we walked to the cart, I fumed. A three-putt had *not* been my plan. My first putt should have been easy, leaving me with a bogey. Now I had a triple bogey—all because those other players had distracted me. Crappy putting is not typical of me, I rationalized. I should have sunk it in one, easily—two putts, without a doubt.

"I'm not counting that first putt," I told my husband. "I was all stressed out about those guys and I wasn't focused on my game. If I had tried, I easily could have sunk it in two shots."

"OK," replied my husband, "let's just lie for fun."

"I'm not lying," I said. "I didn't take my time."

"You should have. We're not playing slow. You need to relax about that other group. And you took three putts. You should count three putts."

"Yeah, but I wasn't paying attention," I continued, though my argument was running out of steam.

"Have you *ever* missed a putt from that distance?" asked Sherlock Holmes.

"Yeah, but not for a long time. I could've made this one."

"But you didn't," he said, looking me in the eyes. Then he looked away. "I don't care. Count your score however you want."

I took the triple bogey out of guilt but was still unhappy about it. I know I could have sunk that putt, but the fact is: I didn't. Sometimes that's just the way the golf ball rolls. I'm sure Tiger Woods can recount a few shots he could have played better if not for a screaming baby sounding off during his backswing or a camera flash exploding in his face. The rules of golf say each shot counts. And all shots do.

So, rule No. 1 in golf is: You must count *every* shot. That means *every single swing* at the ball, even if you miss (you read it right). If you attempt to hit a ball but fail to make contact, you gotta add a stroke to your score. A mulligan, which is a second attempt off the tee box, is not an automatic do-over. In a friendly game, you may take a mulligan if the other players agree, but in a tournament, when establishing your handicap, or during any round in which you want an accurate score, you may *not* take mulligans and you *must* count every single stinkin' hit.

Now, I may jeopardize a few friendships by saying this, but I believe some gals have, shall we say, "flexible" scoring habits. I find this to be mostly true of novice golfers and those who are unfamiliar with the rules. When you don't know the rules and you hit the ball so many times you lose count, it can be pretty hard to keep an accurate score. I've been guilty of this. When I first started playing golf, I played three or four times a year—usually when friends or family were in town or when my husband and I went on vacation. I was, in every sense, a novice with little consistency in my game.

"Oh, I probably score in the 110 to 115 range," I guessed one night at a party. I figured 110 was about right, nothing amazing, but a nice, honest score.

"That's not too bad," replied a friend. "That's what I shoot, and I play more often. Hey, we should get the guys and play eighteen together sometime. We'd probably be an even match."

"Sounds fun," I agreed, not knowing the deep, murky predicament I was creating for myself.

Two weeks later, we met our friends for the promised round of golf. "My goal is to break one hundred this year!" I said to my husband as we headed to the first hole.

"Wait, wait, wait," he said. "Have you ever even played every shot on a full eighteen—no mulligans, no picking up your ball, no gimme putts, and counting every single swing?"

"Even counting my misses?" I asked incredulously. (What kind of joke was this?)

"Even your misses. That's the rule," he replied.

"Yikes," I said, not so happy about this rule revelation. "Well, I'll count everything today," I said, thinking that *maybe* I would score closer to a 117 or a 120—since I did tend to swing and miss the ball a few times per round.

Eighteen holes, one hot dog, three Gatorades, and two potty breaks later, it was all I could do to dam the flood of tears about to erupt from my eyes. My scorecard read 139. I felt humiliated.

"I just fell apart today," I said to our friends. "I don't know what happened."

"Don't worry about it," they said graciously. "Everyone has a bad day."

But that was the catch. I didn't have a bad day. The day's round had been a fair representation of my skill. I'd never before kept a true score, and now that I knew how bad I was, it hurt.

I was suffering from what I like to call "flexible scoring-induced delusion." This is a dangerous (and potentially embarrassing) condition in which you believe you are a much better player than you really are. Aside from having actual delusions, the problem with this condition is that you won't be able to walk the walk, and depending on whom you play, if you don't keep score correctly, you may be perceived as a cheater.

Now, I'm no cheater; yet, over the years of casual golf with my hubby, I had developed some bad habits that contributed to my delusional state. I'd gotten in the habit of taking an extra swing if I needed one, picking up my ball when I was frustrated, and not counting my "air-ball" whiffs. While I do recommend picking up to preserve pace of play if you're learning and are already over double par, *when you move into the arena of announcing your score, be sure you know what the rules are, how to play, and how to document your score. Be accurate!*

While I can't help you with your execution, I can help with a few common-knowledge rules and scoring tips. The following are some abbreviated basics that should help you as a new player. If you progress in the game and aspire to play in a league or other competitive environments, you will need to expand your knowledge base. I encourage you to visit the USGA Web site, www.usga.org, and read the official USGA listing of *The Rules of Golf*. The Web site is packed with information, and I recommend it for anyone wanting a better grasp of the game, looking for rules updates, etc.

JUST THE BASICS

OK, here's the scoop: This is a basic outline of the rules that, in my opinion, you would need to know most. This is not a comprehensive or technical listing; it's the simplified basics I've learned while playing the game. Once you have your feet firmly on the fairway, so to speak, you can dive into the specifics on your own.

Count every stroke. This is rule No. 1. Even if you're not in competitive play, counting every stroke will give you a true indication of where your game is and establish good scoring habits. If, like me, you start out with a score of 139 (or higher), keep perspective! I remind myself that I'm a busy mom, still learning, and just playing for fun. (Occasionally my competitive side gives in to my inner Pollyanna perspective, and I enjoy myself, despite my performance. Other times, I consider myself seriously warped for playing the game so poorly.)

Make sure you can identify your ball. If you cannot remember what type of ball you're playing, mark it. Keep a permanent marker in your bag and personalize your ball with your initials, a heart, or whatever works for you.

Carry no more than 14 clubs in your bag. Whatever your combination of clubs, limit them to 14.

Don't solicit advice on what club to hit. This falls into the category of "husband golf" and can be hazardous to your round and your relationship! Ultimately, *you* must learn what club to hit from any given spot on the course. If you choose your clubs, you'll discover what clubs to use/not to use; if your partner chooses, you may blame him or her for a poor shot and even fail to gain an understanding of your own game.

If you have a general question, ask it. The friends in your foursome may be a good resource for you as you learn. However, make sure you don't pepper them with questions incessantly—as too many questions can be distracting to *their* game. (You want to be invited back to play with them again, don't you?)

You can take a practice swing, but not a practice stroke. Likewise, one practice swing (two, max!) is sufficient. Practice on the driving range; play on the course. This will preserve pace of play.

If your ball falls off the tee or you knock it off accidentally, there is no penalty. If you have the intent to hit, then the stroke counts.

Play the ball as you find it. This means no touching the ball, no picking it up to wipe the mud off, or bumping it out of a divot to a better place on the fairway. Just hit the ball and do your best.

Play the course as you find it. Don't stomp down the tall weeds in front of your ball to help clear a path, don't bend tree limbs or bushes, etc. Bummer, I know. Until I learned of this, I was majorly guilty of grass stomping. Now, I just select a club with a lot of loft, say a prayer, and swing!

Don't touch the ground in the hazard before you hit. Technically, this is called grounding the club. This rule applies to *all* hazards—sand *and* water. (I've never tried to hit out of a water hazard. I can't imagine wading in after a ball or leaning over a pond to take a shot. I'm too clumsy and prefer to take the penalty rather than provide comic relief for my group as I fish frogs out of my shorts. If you're really brave and hit out of the water, I applaud your effort.)

If you play the wrong ball (no, no, no!), you must take a two-stroke penalty and then play your own ball. This adds up quickly, so pay attention!

Taking a drop. Stretch your arm out and drop the ball, don't place it.

Lost balls and out-of-bounds. If you *know* your ball is lost out-of-bounds (e.g., you see it fly over a fence and bounce across a city street), then replay the shot and add a penalty stroke to your score.

Water hazards. If you hit into a water hazard, you have a couple of options: 1) take your next shot from behind the water at the spot where the ball went into the hazard and take a penalty stroke, and 2) hit another ball from the spot where you took your first shot and take a penalty stroke. The most common way to play this is option No. 1. I usually find where the ball entered the water and hit another ball, counting my score like this: "In the water one, out two (the penalty stroke), hitting three."

On the putting green. You may remove rocks, sand, leaves, and other loose obstructions from your line of putt with your club or hand. It is very important to note that once you're on the putting green, *it is a two-stroke penalty if your ball hits the pin!* Translation: If you chip onto the green and the ball rolls in the hole with the flag still in place, *Wahoo!* Good shot! But, if you're already on the green and sink your first putt with the flag still in the hole, *you must take a two-stroke penalty.* Boo-hoo, big bummer! So remember, once you're on the green, have someone tend the flag or pull it out of the cup before you putt.

Unplayable ball. The main thing to remember here is that you have options. You judge (Girl Scout's honor) whether your ball is unplayable at any point on the course. If you declare a ball unplayable, you have three options: 1) take your next shot from the spot where you hit your first ball; 2) hit a new ball from within two club lengths of the spot, but not any closer to the hole (i.e., to the side or behind the unplayable lie); and 3) hit from an imaginary line behind the ball, in line with the hole, as far back as you wish.

WEIRD STUFF

There is a ball-stealing fox that lives around the sixth hole on my home course. The course actually has a sign that advises using an old ball on No. 6 because if the fox sees your ball, he'll snatch it! No kidding! So, what's the rule if the fox (or a clueless golfer) picks up your ball and takes off with it? You may replace the ball in the same spot without penalty. Here are a few other weird circumstances that might occur:

Ground under repair or standing water on the course. If your ball lies in an area of the fairway that is under repair or water sodden, or in a gopher hole, you may drop without penalty within one club length of the nearest point of relief, but not any closer to the hole.

Moveable obstructions. If you need to move something out of the way to hit your ball, you may do so without penalty (as long as the obstruction is not attached to the ground—no uprooting plants or breaking anything). An example that comes to mind is, if your ball comes to rest underneath the string that closes off an area of the course, you may pull up the stake and lay it on the ground, hit, and then replace the stake/string.

Other obstructions. If you can't move an object and it's blocking your swing, then you may need to take an unplayable lie.

The cart path is your friend. If your ball lands on, or you need to stand on the cart path in order to hit, you may play it as is or take a free drop within one club length. (You can drop the ball to the side or behind, not forward toward the pin. Use your driver to measure; it's your longest club.)

Local rules. Many golf courses have rules that apply only to that specific course. These are usually noted on the scorecard or reviewed by the starter prior to your round. Pay attention to these rules, as they may vary and are course specific.

SCORING

Once you know the rules, then scoring will be a piece of cake, right? Wrong. As if there weren't enough to remember already, with what to bring, how to swing, terminology, and rules, now you must count your score correctly. As I mentioned before, when you first learn the game, sometimes it's hard to keep track of all your strokes. If you're hitting the ball twice as much as others in your group and becoming frustrated while trying to focus on getting to the green, it can be easy to forget a shot—or lose count completely—as you make your journey down the fairway.

Golf is a game of honor. You may be a person of great integrity, but if you can't keep track of your score, you may not seem all that honorable. It cannot be overstated: scoring accuracy is extremely important, and you must keep proper track of your shots. If you're having trouble, purchase a little score tracker that clips onto your belt. Each time you take a shot, click the score tracker—and when you finish the hole, or "hole out," your scorecard will be accurate.

Make a mental note of each swing. For example: *I hit my tee shot. I am laying one, hitting two. I am laying two, hitting three. I am laying three, hitting four. I am laying four, putting five. The ball is in the hole. I have a five on this hole.* As my time playing the game has increased and my average number of shots per hole has decreased, I've gotten much better at tracking my score. But this isn't something to take lightly. Accurate scoring is of paramount importance.

Here are some key pointers on keeping an accurate score:

- Know the rules and play by them.
- Score penalty shots accurately.
- Purchase a score tracker, wear it, and use it.
- Make a careful mental note of your score as you take each shot.
- Document accurately on your scorecard.

• Be honest, even if it hurts. Remember: your score does not define you; it's just a record of a particular round on a particular day.

SCORECARD

Before you begin your round, make sure to look over the scorecard. Pay attention to what par is for each hole, the yardage for each hole, and the handicap rating. The handicap rating is the difficulty rating of each hole on the course. For example, the hole with the 1 listed under Handicap is the hardest hole on the course; the hole listed as 18 is the easiest. Next, locate the spot on the card where you record scores. Make sure you don't start writing scores too early, or too late—by the time you discover this error, it may be difficult to make corrections. When you finish each hole, go to the next tee box, then record your score.

Although the scorecard seems fairly straightforward, here are a few tips:

• When playing with a handicap, the dots in each box are the strokes given on each hole. For example, if my handicap is a 10, I might get two shots on the three hardest holes and one shot each on the next four most difficult holes.

Rule Ramblings

1. Ignorance of the rules was my excuse
2. Hazards: A test of skill —not always a bad thing
3. Out-of-bounds, but not out of control
4. Never keep score in life—just in golf
5. Save that outstanding scorecard, and like your first dollar earned: Frame it!

(The dots indicate the extra strokes you are given on a particular hole—so you subtract these from your total score at the end of the round.)

• Draw a square around a bogey.

• Leave a par as is. Hooray!

• Draw a circle around a birdie!

• And for an eagle? Mark it with a triangle. Then throw your scorecard in the air, whoop with joy, and gloat!

Rules and scoring can be tough, and once you learn the rules—and accurately track your score—it can even be painful (to your ego). When you first start, I suggest playing a few rounds without trying to keep score in order to minimize frustration and discouragement. Once you progress in your game, then keep track of your score accurately. Hang on to your score-cards. Though you may start with a humiliating 139, you will see improvement as time passes, especially if you start with a score like mine. This is one of the most rewarding aspects of the sport and part of what keeps bringing us back.

Keep your head up (as long as you're not hitting), be honest, and just play. Keep in mind that some courses are more difficult than others. A 105 on a really tough course may be the score equivalent of a 97 on an easier course. A score is a number written on a piece of paper. You are not your score; you are so much more.

No Chitchat During the Backswing
Etiquette

If you drink, don't drive. Don't even putt.
— Dean Martin

I'M ON THE dance floor. I am a rock star!" I sing enthusiastically after I chip a shot onto the green from 40 yards out. The other players in my group cannot hear my boastful jingle, they're scattered around the fairway, finishing their own shots. Even though my haughty little tune isn't intended for their ears, it's a good thing they can't hear me; my singing is as bad as my golf.

I grab my clubs and walk the short distance to the green. As I approach, I see four balls scattered around at varying distances from the hole. I look at the first ball; it's not mine. As I make my way to check the second ball, Pete, my husband, moans as if his appendix has burst.

"Uh, Celeste, you just walked across my line."

"Your what? I was just trying to figure out which ball was mine."

"Well, watch where you're going. You need to make sure you don't step on anyone's putting line."

"Oh, sorry." I feel like I'm being reprimanded by my dad for spilling a soda. It was an honest mistake, but I make a mental note to pay better attention to what I'm doing—and where I'm walking—especially on the green.

On the next green, I am very careful to avoid stepping on anyone's line. I'm closer to the hole than the other players but across the green from my ball. So, as each player gets ready to putt, I walk around the perimeter of the green to avoid accidentally committing another line-stepping faux pas.

"What are you doing?" my husband asks, looking at me as if I'm missing a few divots in my fairway.

"I'm going to my ball."

"Why are you walking back there? Just go straight to your ball."

"But I don't want to step on anyone's line," I say, circling the green like a tourist looping Big Ben.

"So step over it," he says.

I'm in trouble again. What's next, restriction? Will my telephone privileges be revoked? Or will I just be suspended from playing golf with my friends?

A few holes later, I'm not sure what to do. Two players have their golf balls very close to each other. If I go straight to my ball, per my husband's advice, I may disturb one of their "lines." Even if I step over their imaginary routes, I feel I may encroach on their putting area. So I summon my inner dancer and perform a split leap—over both putting lines.

OK, maybe I won't get a casting call from *Fame*, but I land right near my ball and am impressed with my graceful, soft-spike landing. This must be why they call it the "dance floor"—because sometimes you have to pull out a strategic ballroom move to negotiate the green.

"That was pretty," says one player, chuckling.

"What was *that*?" asks my husband. He looks horrified, as though I've just insulted his boss.

"It was a split leap," I tell him. I have again breached etiquette, but I'm trying my best to get it right. I'm embarrassed, but I don't feel too foolish; after all, it *was* a pretty good split leap. Anyone who had seen *Dancing with the Stars* could at least appreciate that.

What a nightmare. Though proper etiquette seems to be common sense, it can be very confusing for someone new to the game. Knowing and remembering the subtle nuances of etiquette is tricky—and as a beginner, hard to understand. Come on. Can a mark from my shoe really screw up someone's putt? If my putts were so precise that an indention in the green (from a shoe!) could throw my ball off course, I'd be playing in the LPGA. For all I care, the entire Norman High School Band could have a "drill down" on my line; it wouldn't affect my game. Still, beginning golfer or not, etiquette guidelines must be followed by all players.

WHY ETIQUETTE?

Why is etiquette important? And what does it mean for you and me? It means that if we choose to pick up a club, we are responsible to respect others, show courtesy for their game, know the rules, and play in the spirit of good sportsmanship. This is easier said than done.

Even when I knew not to step on someone's putting line, I debated the proper way to get to my ball. Do I go around the edge of the green? Walk straight to it? If I go straight and need to step over someone's line, how much room do I need to have on each side? One inch? Four inches? A foot?

Obviously, based on my experience, a leap is not required—and in retrospect, I can't recall ever seeing a khaki-clad male golfer spring forcefully across the green to his ball—but frustration and heat can make one do strange things.

Though you, too, may occasionally channel Martha Graham, the golf course is not the best place to bust a move. Save your moves for Ladies Night. Being aware of and adhering to proper etiquette demonstrates respect for other players, helps ensure the safety of all individuals, keeps up the pace of the game, and preserves the condition of the course.

THE BASICS OF ETIQUETTE

The following are the basics of golf etiquette. This list is not all-encompassing, but it
does cover most of what you'll need to know.

Keep quiet

The importance of keeping quiet while
other players hit cannot be overstated. (This is
why I'm leading with this tip and repeat it
throughout the book.) When someone is hitting, whether teeing off, in the middle of the
fairway, or putting, keep quiet. Golf requires a
lot of concentration, and having people chat—
or even whisper—while you try to swing is akin
to taking the SAT in a day-care center.

As a beginner you may have questions; ask
them later. As a busy woman you may not get
many chances to catch up with friends; meet
prior to your round for some coffee-chat. Though
small noises may not bother you, they can
upset many golfers, so be respectful of all players by maintaining silence while everyone hits.

Though chitchat is the most common
offense, be aware that in the midst of a backswing, any noise can be distracting. This
includes popping the brake on the golf cart,

blowing your nose, opening a soda can, rattling a chip bag, or having a cell phone ring. Hopefully, when it's your turn to hit, others will accord you the same respect.

When you hit

When you swing your club, the goal is to get the ball into the hole—not make a hole in the side of someone's head. Keep this in mind at all times; never swing a club when someone is walking or standing close by. (And always make sure *you* don't walk too close to someone else either!)

Never tee off (or hit) when the group in front of you is within the distance you are capable of hitting the ball. If you think there is even a chance you might hit someone with your ball, warn them before you swing. When I first started playing the game, this meant alerting any players standing nearby! If you hit a ball that looks like it might possibly hit someone, yell, "Fore!" as loudly as you can. This is the customary warning to let others know a wayward ball may be heading toward them.

Keep on movin'

An important part of etiquette is keeping up

the pace of play. Be ready to hit when it's your turn. Don't take a zillion practice swings before hitting; practice at the driving range, play on the course. Don't spend more than two to three minutes searching for a lost ball. If you seem to lose a lot of balls but still love to play, then buy golf balls on sale or ask for them for your birthday, Christmas, and other holidays. (I have seen used recycled balls—of various brands—in a mesh bag for sale at some stores. I'm sure you can find good deals like this if you keep you eyes open.)

Cut the socializing and focus on the game. If the group behind you is waiting on your group, consider letting them play through. Maintaining proper pace of play is important for everyone. It can be tedious to wait for a certain player—or a group in front of you—time and time again, plus finishing a round on time may give you a chance to have an iced tea and relax in the clubhouse before you rush home to pay the sitter.

Just like Dad's car

When I was a youngster, it was an unwritten rule that when we rode in Dad's car, we had to keep French-fry fingers off the leather, never shove gum wrappers into the ashtray, and always pick up all our stuff when we arrived home. Dad liked to keep his cars nice, and by doing so, he taught us respect for the property of others. Treat the golf course like a nice car; respect it. Though you may have paid a hefty greens fee, you do not own the course. You have merely paid for the privilege to play.

Make sure you pick up your trash, repair divots and ball marks, and be careful to prevent damage to the course at all times. This means that if you shank a shot, it is not OK to pound your club into the ground. It also means you must adhere to the rules pertaining to where and how to drive the golf cart, as well as obeying any local rules that are course specific. (Local rules are usually reviewed by the course starter and/or listed on the scorecard.)

On the green

I find the putting green can be an arena for etiquette embarrassment. As noted earlier, when I first started the game, I was a mess on the green. Now that I've figured out what to do (and what not to do), here are a few tips for when you, too, are on the dance floor. (Ironic isn't it? A dance floor with no dancing allowed!)

When you get to the green, walk straight to your ball without stepping on someone's line to get to it. (Their "line" is the imaginary line from their ball to the hole.) You don't need to leap; a simple step over the area will suffice. If you're not sure where their ball will break, or are otherwise worried you might encroach on someone's line, avoid the area and take the next shortest route to your ball.

Once you get to your ball, mark it. (As I mentioned in Chapter 3, in a friendly game, you may not need to mark your ball unless it's blocking another player's putt, but traditionally you always mark your ball.) Whoever is farthest out will putt first. Discreetly plan your shot while others putt; if you are to the left or right of a player's line of sight, stand back and give them some room.

Though it would be oh so helpful, do not squat behind them to "read" their putt (see how their ball breaks on the green) so as to properly strategize your own putt. Give players adequate room. Once you have "holed out," pick up your ball and wait for the others to finish.

The last important thing to make note of on the putting green is what I like to call the "five o'clock shadow." This is not the scruffy accumulation of facial hair a man has by day's end, but the long shadow that falls across someone's putting line from a player not paying attention. While shadows can occur most any time of day, I notice they are longest—and I am most forgetful—in the late afternoon or early evening after a long day.

"Do you want me to tend the hole?" I ask, trying to be helpful. I am not putting; I have already doubled par and picked up my ball. This is just a practice round for me.

"Sure, that'd be great," says my friend. She chips up to the green, but her ball is still a fair distance from the hole.

"Do you need the flag?" I ask her.

"Not anymore, thanks," she says. I pull the pin and then step away from the hole. My friend sets up to putt, pauses, then looks at me, slightly frustrated. "Can you move? Your shadow is on my line."

Though I feel I am far enough away from her, my long late-day shadow stretches across the green, covering her route to the hole. "Oops. Sorry," I say, jumping back.

It's an easy mistake to make. However, a putt must be precise, and sometimes shadows or divots from a shoe spike can make or break a tricky putt. Pay attention to where you stand on the green.

Lookin' good on the green

What you wear is considered part of proper etiquette. You should generally try to dress conservatively—think longer shorts instead of shorter ones—and classic styles are better than something really outlandish. A collared shirt is standard for most courses.

I have a friend, bless her misguided heart, who wears the most absurd hats when she plays golf. I hate to say it, but she looks ridiculous. Ladies, this is not the Kentucky Derby. Baseball caps, visors, and simple bucket hats are good options to keep the sun off your face and head. Leave the floppy-brimmed straw hats—and anything with a silk flower on it—at home. (Come to think of it, you may want to leave the silk flowers at the store.)

When you're getting dressed, remember to wear something comfortable. Shorts that ride up your butt and too-tight waistbands are no fun after five hours on the golf course.

Last of all, you must wear pants or shorts

with pockets. I know that pockets—especially pockets crammed with golf balls, tees, and other items—are not exactly slimming, but the golf course is not the place to try to convince people you could be a body double for Elle McPherson. You might look bulky, but if that bothers you, put on your "skinny" jeans and have a Slim Fast when you get home.

When the rules bend

While the rules of etiquette never bend with regard to safety, respect for others, and course maintenance, they sometimes vary with what you may wear. I have seen someone play golf shirtless and another play 18 holes in sandals (not recommended). I also know someone who had a hole-in-one while pregnant, wearing short denim overalls and tennis shoes. Overalls and tennis shoes! Can you believe it? How hideous! Um, yeah, that was me.

(Hey, cut me some slack, I *was* wearing a collared shirt, even if it was one of my husband's, and I had to cram it under my overalls around my pregnant belly. Talk about bulky! The golf balls in your pocket don't seem too bad now, do they?)

While I don't recommend golfing without your shirt on—though some of the male contingent in your foursome might approve—I tell you these stories to illustrate that not all golf facilities have the same attire protocol. Some golf centers are fairly lax. A family fun center, for example, might allow you to wear a regular shirt and/or tennis shoes. Many public courses allow tennis shoes; most private courses and clubs do not. If you are not sure, the best thing to do is call the course and check what attire is appropriate.

When I played in my denim overalls, I wondered why the women in the locker room turned their noses up at me. I thought they were snobs. *I was unaware that my attire was inappropriate*; no one ever said a word. My guess is, the staff in the pro shop probably felt sorry for me—and couldn't bear to send the fat pregnant lady home to change. It's a good thing too. With the explosive mix of hormones and humidity I was experiencing that day, I probably would have had a tearful breakdown in the women's merchandise section.

So on occasion, the rules might bend. Since you have the benefit of this handy book, you will not have to subject yourself to such humili-ation. Prior to your round you can run over to the mall and pick up some khaki maternity shorts and a hip mom-to-be Polo. You'll look and feel much better when you make your lucky hole-in-one!

If you are pregnant or have other physical limitations, you may be given flexibilities in a friendly round. For example, while it is customary for all players to "hole out" before leaving the putting green, there are excep-tions. Pregnant or elderly people needing a rest or wanting to escape the heat may sit in the cart while the others finish the hole. By the same token, if the rest-rooms are nearby and your bladder is

Emily Post would be proud!

Five rules of golf etiquette

1. No dancing on the dance floor
2. When someone is swing-ing ..."Shhhh!"
3. Keep up the pace
4. Repair divot marks—yours and one more!
5. Don't step on someone's putting line (or their foot)

so full you cannot stand up straight (a definite physical limitation), then it's acceptable to putt out and zip off the green for a potty break. Only you know the type of game you are playing and what your needs are. Various instances like this may come up over the course of a round. Listen to your body and take care of yourself. If it's a competitive round and you can wait a few minutes to take care of your needs, then wait for an appropriate time.

Still, make your health and welfare (and that of others) priority No. 1. Just as proper etiquette says you should not tee off until you're sure the golfers ahead of you are out of range, it's important to make sure that if you feel sick or dizzy—or you think someone in your group does—you attend to those needs. Heatstroke and dehydration are as dangerous on the course as getting nailed in the head by a golf ball.

And don't forget to enjoy your game. While this may seem like a lot to remember, you will eventually learn it all. Grasp the main concepts and do your best. You just might have the shot of the day.

How to Succeed as a Mom and a Golfer

It is almost impossible to remember how tragic a place the world is when one is playing golf.

— Robert Lynd

I CANNOT FIND a sitter for the baby, so I guess I'll have to stay home."

"But didn't you want to play today, Honey?"

"Yeah, I really want to play, but I have no other option unless you stay home and I go golf with your dad and brother."

My husband doesn't even respond to this suggestion. I knew he wouldn't. I just threw it out to make a point about maternal sacrifice. He, the dad, pass up a day of golf? *Not* an option.

"Well, we could bring her."

"Bring her? That's a brilliant idea. I'm sure they let babies on the course all the time."

"Seriously, we can bring her," my husband says, trying to convince me. "No one will even know she's with us. She'll probably sleep in her car seat the whole time. "

"You think she'll stay asleep for four and a half hours?"

"Well, she's been in a car that long and done all right."

"What if she gets hit by a golf ball?"

"Oh, relax, she'll be fine. Dad and Taylor can help keep an eye on her. I'm sure it will be no big deal."

Problem No. 1 is that I listened to my husband. While he is very intelligent and often lends a helpful perspective to tough situations, this is neither his lightbulb moment— nor mine.

For the round that day, I pack my golf bag with tees, balls, and bottles of milk. When we arrive at the course, I stay in the car with our infant while my husband loads our clubs onto a cart and pays the greens fee. Then he comes to pick us up. We pull the car seat, with baby asleep inside, out of the base and nestle it between us on the cart bench. I toss a sweat-shirt over the car seat and we head to the first hole. We won't be hitting practice balls this round.

As we near the starter, I panic. *He'll see the baby. He'll kick us off the course. I knew this was a bad idea. What was I thinking?* My husband drives the cart like Jeff Gordon in the final lap of a NASCAR race. As we pass the starter, I know I need to distract him from the stowaway in our cart. So, with a white-knuckle grip on the car seat, I turn sideways to block his view of the baby. I wave with my free hand, flashing the biggest smile I can muster.

"Have fun out there," he says.

"Oh, I'm sure I'll have fun," I reply.

And so we're off. I head to the first tee with an extra ball—and a pacifier—in my pocket. I have a spectacular drive off the tee box. We have successfully duped the starter, and my ball is on the fairway. Maybe this will work out after all.

"Fore!"

The voice booms out of nowhere. We all look up to locate the errant ball, and as we do, it bounces off the ground a few feet from us, landing right by our cart.

"Oh my gosh, that ball could have hit the baby!" I say, more freaked out than I had been in childbirth.

"It was nowhere near her," says Mr. Calm. "She's fine."

The baby may be fine, but I'm not. After the incident, I can't focus on my game. I don't want to be more than a few feet from the cart and do not trust the rest of my family foursome with the supervision of the baby. They're tuned into their game, not the sleepy six-month-old nestled in our golf cart. I don't last past the fourth hole. I take the baby and go home—which is the first good decision of the day.

Being a mom is hard. When children are young, caring for them is physically exhausting: midnight feedings, diapers, and attending to every need leaves us bushed. Often after a long day of work and caring for my children, I want to sneak into a bath or crawl under my covers, not to be disturbed for hours. Yet, as soon as the house is quiet and the opportunity for a bit of relaxation appears, a child will wake up crying from a nightmare—or the water heater will burst. Either way, I'm running once again. Older children can take care of their own needs, but alas, they can be even more mentally draining. They challenge us and push us to our limits as they develop a sense of self and discover just what they can get away with.

Sacrifice is intrinsic to parenting. Without being patronizing or preachy, I will say that being a parent is the hardest, most noble job anyone can do. Many men are Mr. Mom, loving, nurturing, and sacrificing for the benefit of their children. But, as a general rule, mothers tend to make a greater *social* sacrifice for their kids. (I'm the one who left the golf course that day, not my husband.)

If someone stays home with the children, it's usually the mom. Men typically have a higher earning capacity, so this makes economic sense for most families. However, working outside the home affords men chances for adult interaction, lunch meetings that consist of more than PB&J, and a tangible reward for their breadwinning efforts. Women who work both outside and at home may enjoy the perks and challenges of a career, but they may be too stressed and overscheduled to enjoy them.

Regardless, most moms are frazzled, over-worked, and just plain tired.

So what does this have to do with golf? It relates in the sense that many moms may feel too busy or too guilty to take time for themselves—and this includes playing golf. Note the operative word *feel*. We *feel* we have too much on our plate and that taking time for ourselves takes away from our children, but that is not necessarily true. Two phrases, though a bit cliché, sum up the important points here: "When mom ain't happy, nobody's happy," and "Where there's a will, there's a way."

When mom ain't happy, nobody's happy is so true. When you're spent, exhausted, and irritable, your family feels it. They just know. When I'm grouchy and need a break, I send out a vibe my husband can sense from miles away.

"Whatcha want to do for dinner, Honey?" he asks, casually.

"I dunno. Is dinner always my responsibility?"

"No. I'll take care of it. I was just wondering if you had something specific in mind. I didn't want to order out if you already had something planned."

"No. I don't care what we do. I'm not really hungry anyway."

"OK, I'll take care of dinner. (Pregnant pause.) What's bothering you?"

"You mean besides the fact that our house is a pit, the laundry is never-ending, I have five hours of work waiting on the computer, I never see my friends anymore, and I'm sick of being a diaper-changing machine? Not much."

When I hit "Overload," everything bothers me. I get so enmeshed in what needs doing and in taking care of the needs of everyone else that I run myself into the ground. Then, instead of appreciating all I have, I become resentful. Women who take time for themselves on a regular basis may be viewed by some as self-indulgent or frivolous, but really, they are smart. We must take care of ourselves.

We must schedule "me" time; that's as important as the trips to the pediatrician, the carpool, and that spreadsheet for work. It is more important than dirty laundry and home-cooked meals. Giving yourself regular breaks, exercise, and time with friends will keep your spirit fresh and help you appreciate yourself and the value you bring to your family and life.

So what kind of break should you take? Do whatever renews your spirit. A mani-pedi is always nice, as is dinner out, but an activity that combines fresh air, friends, and exercise is ideal. What offers that? Golf. If you are reading this book, you likely have a budding interest in the sport.

In addition, while moms of young children are in one of the busiest times of their lives, they also live in an era when they likely have more opportunities to play the links than ever before. They may have colleagues who play the game, may have married a golfer, and likely have more disposable income to pursue the sport than in their single days of eating Top Ramen.

Still, despite the opportunities, many moms shy away from the golf course. Why? In addition to being so overscheduled that they don't even have time for personal breaks, they may fear the humiliation of trying a new sport, doubt they will have time enough to practice and improve, or simply not know where or how to start. Here's where the phrase "Where there's a will, there's a way" comes in. It comes down to this: If you value yourself enough, you will see that taking a break and pursuing a passion is a necessity. It doesn't take away anything from your family; they benefit too. After taking time for yourself, you will be more encouraging and focused—and everyone will reap the rewards. It may take some prioritizing, but it is possible. Moms can be fabulous golfers, but first they have to get on the course. If you have a heart to play, you can find a way.

FRUSTRATION AND PERSPECTIVE

It wasn't until I was a mother of two children, the second only months old, that I got serious about my golf game. I took 25 strokes off my game the summer after my second child was born. Why didn't I do it when I was single and childless? I didn't want it badly enough.

Over the years, I finally got tired of being the weakest player in our vacation foursome, but it was more than that. Time at the driving range became "me time." My infant daughter was so sweet, so cuddly, and so demanding. Coupled with her older sister, who wanted attention and a "dress-up" mannequin, I was exhausted and needed a break. So I recruited a babysitter, and while they napped in the afternoons, I took my break at the driving range.

With each smack of the ball I honed my skill. I gained a sense of control. I found peace and hope in the game I once found exasperating. I wanted more, so I signed up for lessons. And my game improved.

What did parenting teach me that I failed to grasp before having children? Perspective. At one time, playing golf left me feeling inadequate, unworthy, and unskilled. At times parenting also leaves me feeling inadequate and unskilled, but at least it gives my life perspective. Perspective in this context means that when you spend your days changing dirty diapers, heating strained peas, and dealing with tantrums at story time, failing to shoot par doesn't really rattle you.

Golf offers fresh air and a needed break from the daily grind. Any frustration encountered on the course is wiped away like baby food with a paper towel—gone instantly, no big deal. And let's face it, after getting up at 6 a.m. and working all day, you might not swing as well as Phil Mickelson.

Perspective is realizing that parenting does something no job or athletic endeavor can do; it gives us value beyond a critical review or sucky performance. In the overall scheme of things, a shanked hit or a whiffed shot doesn't matter; my kids love me just the same, no matter what I do. (Well, no matter what I do on the golf course. If I come home with the wrong kind of ice cream it's a whole different story.)

Some things are important and some are not. Golf is fun. It offers a challenge, time with friends, and recreation. However, unless you're paid to play the sport—and even if you are— there's a lot more to all of us than how well we swing the clubs.

RAKING THE YARD AND RAKING THE TRAP

"Can I tell you how much I don't want to play in this golf tournament today?" I blurt to my friend, Heather, the instant she picks up the phone.

"Awww, why?" she asks. "It'll be fun."

"I know, but I have so much to do. My purse got stolen at the zoo this weekend, and I need to go to DMV and get a new license. I need to go to the bank and change my account numbers. My family is in town for the next ten days. I'm just overwhelmed. The last thing I can think about is golf."

But I had thought about it; I'd thought about it a lot. I thought about the fact that I'd spent $150 dollars to play in the tournament, a benefit for Children's Hospital. Children's was an organization close to my heart and I wanted to support them. I had also committed to play with my friends. Yet it was a long drive to the club, my to-do list was a mile long, and my swing was rusty—I hadn't played golf in almost six weeks. I knew I had to go to the tournament. I also knew that once I arrived and started to play, I'd have fun. But I couldn't get there mentally; everything in my life seemed much more pressing than an afternoon of golf.

"I'm sorry about your purse," Heather says. "But you should still come; it'll be a good break for you, and I want to see you." I heed the encouragement. It will be nice to spend some time with my girlfriends.

"I'm going to embarrass myself," I say, already making excuses for my game. "I haven't played in forever."

"Who cares? It's just for fun," she reminds me.

"OK, I'll see you there."

I rush around all morning trying to knock out as many errands as possible before I have to depart for the course, leaving just enough cushion to make my tee time. As I pull out of the driveway, I stop short, deciding to leave the stroller for the babysitter. I pull it from the trunk and run it back to the garage. There, I see my golf clubs. In my haste, I'd forgotten to take them ... so typical of my mom-crazed state.

With clubs now on board, I speed along the highway and continue to multitask. While actively scanning for police officers (remember, no driver's license), I eat a banana and an energy bar. I guzzle a bottle of water. Then, with lunch out of the way, I squirt a big blob of sunscreen onto my thigh. Steering the car with one hand, I dab at the blob with my other hand, moving sunscreen from my thigh to my face, neck, chest, arms ... and rubbing the remainder into my legs. Then I register; using my cell phone, I have my friends check me in.

"What color hat do you want?" Erika asks.

"What are my options?"

"Orange, green, blue, and black. I got orange. I think it's the cutest."

"Really?" I ask, thinking I might prefer black. I am never too busy to carefully consider all my options in golf attire.

"Oh, maybe black for you," she says, changing her mind.

"Yeah, get me black," I say. "I'm getting off the highway. I'll be there in ten."

I screech into the parking lot just minutes before the shotgun start. While the bag staff loads my clubs onto the cart, I pull on a visor and locate my friends.

"Let's play!" I exclaim, relieved that I have made it on time—relatively speaking.

"Do you need sunscreen?" Heather asks, offering me her tube.

"Nope, thanks. Already have some on."

"You want a box lunch?" Erika questions.

"Thanks, I already ate," I say. "I'm ready to go." I am a multitasking mom-phenom.

The round proves to be not only fun, but a relaxing break from my frantic day. The scramble format eliminates the pressure to perform. The fresh air clears my mind. The camaraderie is like a long, deep yoga breath, returning my chi to normal levels. The day proves entertaining as well. When Heather nails a house sitting at a 90-degree angle from the tee box, we can't help but giggle. The gentlemen in the foursome behind us thank us for a round of drinks someone else purchased for them. And I, the rusty golfer, hit "Closest to the Pin" on a par- 3 when it counts and win recognition at the post-tournament dinner. I drive home feeling refreshed, inspired, even jubilant. Though my unfinished to-do list greets me when I walk in the door, the time off was well spent, and I attack the chores heartily the next morning.

Although you may never have lost your purse, I'm willing to bet you feel as busy as I do on any given day. Life is busy; schedules fill up. Sometimes, if we're not forced to take a break, we'll go until we break. I wouldn't have played in that tournament, even after paying my registration fee, if my friends had not been counting on me.

The only thing that tipped the scales in favor of going was them. If not for Heather's encouragement, I would have spent the afternoon at the DMV and the grocery store, washing sheets for relatives, and thinking of more things I "had" to do. By day's end, I surely would have been exhausted, irritable, and downright grumpy. And while I know that running myself into the ground is not healthy, I would have done it—because golf somehow feels frivolous, while laundry feels necessary. Plus, when running at such high speeds, we don't tend to look for gas stations until our "Low Fuel" light comes on and we simply run out of gas.

"It doesn't cost any more to keep the top half as full as the bottom," my dad used to tell me when I learned to drive. "When your tank hits the halfway point, stop and fill up." Leave it to my father to dispense such sage advice. It's true, though. You never want to run out of gas—you or your car. So stop and fill up.

Golf counts. Taking time for exercise and relaxation before you break down is healthy, both physically and mentally. If you show your children you have a life beyond them, they will respect you and you will be setting a positive example. Do you want to model resentful drudgery or a healthy balance? Raking the yard can wait. It might be time to rake the trap. (Although getting on the green, avoiding both the yard and the trap, is the best option.)

Since we've covered the topics of purses and laundry, I have to fill you in on one last interesting tidbit: Once you take up golf, you will find golf tees everywhere, and I do mean *everywhere.* If you're doing laundry and check the pockets of your shorts—aha!—you'll find a few golf tees. If you're in the drive-thru at Burger King, digging for a quarter at the bottom of your purse, you may not find any change, but you will find … yes, a golf tee.

I'm not sure how tees make the transition from golf course to bathroom vanity, but someday I daresay you will find a few golf tees nestled down next to your mascara and blush. I've found golf tees in my silverware drawer, my filing cabinet, and my pantry. Go figure. Though they do add to the ever-growing clutter in my home, those golf tees are a constant reminder to get out on the course and play.

BABYSITTERS AND OTHER ACES

"Just get a sitter and we can play on Saturday afternoon."

"OK, sounds good," I say. "See you Saturday."

Just get a sitter. It seems so simple, but the thought of finding someone to watch my children often throws me into a state of "babysitter paralysis." You know what I'm talking about: the sickening fear that renders us unable to pick up the phone.

What if the sitter is careless and shakes the baby? What if she invites her boyfriend over and ignores the children? What if there is an accident?

I envision returning home to hyperactive kids and chaos. This anxious state of paranoia persists until Friday afternoon, when the threat of not finding a sitter outweighs my inaction. I have to find a babysitter or I can't play golf. Yet now it's too late to call. Who waits until Friday afternoon to find a sitter for Saturday? I'm embarrassed to call the few contacts I have, certain they already have plans, not wanting them to hear the desperation in my voice.

"Can you watch the kids?" I ask my husband, knowing he already has plans.

"No, I'm playing in the club championship and can't miss it. I thought you were going to hire a sitter."

So much easier said than done. When I finally muster up the nerve to call, my fears are realized: Everyone I ask is busy. I call my friend and reschedule golf for the following Saturday, when my husband can take the kids. I end up spending my afternoon at Chuck E. Cheese, kicking myself for not planning ahead.

Sound familiar? I'm willing to bet you've missed more than golf for lack of someone to watch your kids. It's tough. Not only must we find someone we trust, they must be available when we need them. We must let go of the unreasonable fear that our kids will suffer if we leave the house for a few hours—and that's not so easy to do either.

When I resigned from my career to stay home with my children, my boss told me, "Everyone is replaceable." Ouch. His comment deflated my ego, but it gave me the freedom to leave without guilt. Was I a good employee? Yes. Would they be able to fill my position? Yes. The same is true for our parenting duties. Now, don't get me wrong. Nobody could ever replace you as a mom on a permanent basis. But can a skilled caregiver fill your shoes for an after-noon? You betcha.

Here's what you need to do: First, acknowl-edge that you need a competent caregiver on a regular basis and be willing to pay for quality care. Whether you want to play golf, get your hair highlighted, or go on a date with your man, if you have children you will need backup at some point. If you lack family or a friend who loves to take your kids when you need them to, you will have to pay for a sitter.

Be willing to pay well. You never want to go cheap on toilet paper, birth control, or babysitters. If a good sitter feels she is paid well and likes your family, she'll probably make the effort to be available when you need her. If you're trying to save a buck and hire someone for less, one of two things will happen: 1) If the sitter is good, she'll drop you as soon as another person offers more money; or 2) a budget sitter will not be the attentive, loving person you want to watch your children. With caregivers, you get what you pay for—and remember, this person is replacing *you*. What would you want to be paid? Think about that.

Second, build a database of sitters you trust. Note the word *database*; a database is a list of names and numbers of *quality contacts*, not the names of two 12-year-olds down the street. Some good ways to find quality sitters are to ask friends and other moms for recommendations, look for part-time help through a nanny service or related Web site, and ask at church, school, dance class, or any other community activity where there are a lot of children. Interview potential caregivers. Set detailed expectations.

I found a caregiver to help me watch my girls over the summer, and she was everything I could have asked for. She loved the kids, played with them, helped keep messes at bay, and was always on time. Yet on her second to last day, I happened to come home as she was making the kids' lunch—microwaving Spaghetti-O's in a plastic container. Yikes! I had a strong conviction against microwaving anything in plastic—and she'd likely been doing it all summer. Was that her fault? Nope. It was mine for failing to set up adequate guidelines for mealtimes and food preparation. If given proper instruction, most good caregivers will do exactly what you need and want them to do.

Third, plan ahead and call your babysitter in advance. This one is logical. The sooner you call, the less likely the sitter will have conflicts and the better chance you'll have to find someone else if your first choice can't do it.

Last of all, remember that you can't control everything. Just like you must hit the ball and hope it lands where you want, you must make an educated choice of a sitter and hope she will supervise your kids as well you would. She probably will. You just have to trust that your kids will be all right for the time you are away, and live your life. If you learn to let go a little bit now, just think how much easier it will be on their first day of kindergarten and when they leave for college.

Having a good babysitter is like having an ace in your back pocket. She is always there when you need her, and she'll be the perfect addition to your full house—as you duck out the door to the golf course. And if you hit an ace on the course while you're there—you'll have to buy drinks in the bar. I guess no matter how great they are, you always pay for your aces, one way or another.

HOW TO PLAY PREGNANT

I made a hole-in-one when I was pregnant with my first child. When I was pregnant with my second, I played regularly until I was eight and a half months along.

"How do you do it?" friends would ask. "Doesn't your stomach get in the way?"

My answer: "Aren't half the men playing golf more pregnant than me?"

I mean no disrespect, but seriously, many of the guys I see on the course have bigger bellies than I did. My swing was not affected all that much—unless I had to hit from a weird angle leaning over the edge of a sand trap—in fact, at times, my game seemed to improve. How do you play pregnant? Heed the following precautions and then … just play.

Consult your physician before you play. If you have been playing regularly when you get pregnant, make sure it is all right to keep playing. Follow the advice of a professional you trust.

Stay hydrated on the course. Drink plenty of fluids, and if you need a break, take one. (Dehydration can be a factor in premature labor.) Remember, the baby is the most important consideration here. And get used to adjusting your lifestyle. When the baby is born, more than your golf game will be affected.

Wear cool clothing, and avoid denim overalls. The cool clothing will keep you from overheating. And avoiding overalls … well, that will just keep you "cool."

Pay extra-special attention on the course. You never want to get hit by a club or a wayward ball, especially when you are (excuse the expression) such a big target. When I was pregnant, my stomach stuck straight out and I had a hard time getting used to it. I was like Mrs. No Depth Perception on *Saturday Night Live* and had to be especially careful of others when on the driving range or tee box.

Consider attaching a little suction cup to the end of your putter. This can be a big help when your back starts to hurt from bending over to get your ball out of the hole. The creaky old ladies in my league use these too. After they putt out, they just flip over their putter and suction the ball right out of the cup. I never had one of these, but if I got pregnant again, I'd get one for sure.

Be gentle with yourself. Listen to your body and remember your health is paramount. One person might play regularly, go into labor on the course, and deliver the next Tiger Woods on the 18th hole. Another might not feel up to playing golf after a few months of pregnancy and stay at home with her feet up. Do what feels best for you and enjoy this time while you can. Remember, they call it labor for a reason—and I'm not just referring to childbirth.

You can succeed as a mom-golfer. You really can; however, it takes a bit more work and planning. You must make the time, schedule a sitter, and pay for more than just greens fees. Still, you might have a bit more perspective and be less easily frustrated than other golfers when your game goes south. It all evens out in the end. Sure, other golfers may have a better swing and more leisure time to practice, but they might not hear enthusiastic screams of *"Mommy! Mommy!"* coupled with a cornucopia of hugs and kisses greeting them at the door either.

Secrets of a Mom-Golfer

1. If your husband has the time, so do you
2. Have a backup babysitter
3. Turn your carpet into a putting green (and your toddler into your caddie)
4. Take-out is your friend
5. A double-bogey beats laundry any day

THE BOYS CLUB

If you think it is hard to meet new people,
try picking up the wrong golf ball.

— Jack Lemmon

"HEY LOOK! I found a ball."

I glance over to see my friend picking a ball off the fairway as if she is a child carelessly plucking a dandelion from her front yard.

"Oh, I wouldn't do that," I say.

I start to tell her to leave the ball alone, yet even as I speak, a golf cart bounds over the hill. Two older male golfers are in the cart, zigging this way and that, panning the area for their wayward ball.

"Have you seen a Titleist Number One?" asks the passenger in the cart.

My friend looks down at her hand. "Here it is. I just found it!" she squeals delightedly and saunters over to him, slapping the ball into his palm.

"You picked it up?" he asks incredulously. He is more than a bit irritated. My friend is silent. She looks crestfallen; she's not sure what to say or what she did wrong.

"Sorry," I tell them, shrugging my shoulders. "This is her first day golfing and she's still learning the ropes. Your ball was right here." I walk over and indicate the spot where my friend disturbed their game. The men don't reply; they merely mumble profanities and shake their heads.

We walk away quickly. "You can't do that," I tell her. "Never pick up someone else's ball."

"Well, I didn't know it was theirs. And they weren't very nice. They should've been nicer— at least I found it."

"Yeah, but they could have found it on their own," I tell her. "You never want to move another ball on the course. It's just the way it is. Just play your own ball and leave the others alone, OK?"

This is the kind of thing guys hate, and frankly, I understand. It can be extremely frustrating to lose a $4 golf ball in the rough, but to have a fellow golfer steal it from the edge of the fairway is even worse. My friend didn't know proper protocol, so perhaps it was my fault; I neglected to mention this tidbit of information in my pre-round brief. Still, though rare, instances like this can give us girls a bad rap.

When you play the game, you must know the rules. When you play with the men—and you will—you need to be especially attuned to the way they play, what their habits are, and what irritates them most. For many guys who grow up playing golf, there is a lot of tradition associated with the game. We should respect that. We have every right to be on the course with them, but some insight into their mind-set can make the game more enjoyable for all players and protect the reputation of all the Women on the Green.

THE SATURDAY SNEAK
One male phenomenon is what I like to call the "Saturday Sneak." Ever since I've known my husband, he has been an attentive mate,

interested in shared activities, spending time with me whenever I want—except on Saturdays. For him, Saturdays and golf are like pizza and beer: you can't have one without the other. At first I didn't begrudge him his weekend golf outings—I had my own plans and interests— and at times, I'd join him on the course. Yet, once we had children, I began to resent his unwavering dedication to the game.

Even when I was breast-feeding a newborn, he'd schedule golf a week in advance and disappear before dawn every Saturday. His standard line was, "I would *much* rather be home with you and the baby, but I've already committed to the guys and can't miss my tee time." Yeah right. All the guys were in on this Saturday Sneak, leaving behind girlfriends, wives, children, and responsibilities to converge on the course for an early morning game of skins.

In her book *The Girlfriends' Guide to Getting Your Groove Back,* Vicki Iovine calls golf the "anti-parent." When you're talking about dads and the Saturday Sneak, she is right on target:

Fresh air, athleticism, and male bonding are pretty hard to find fault with. I just have one teeny tiny problem with the golf epidemic among the daddy ranks: Do you realize that it takes a minimum of five hours to finish playing 18 holes?

It's as if an entire generation of responsible fathers got a doctor's note to sneak out of the house long before the breakfast rush and hide out on the rolling links throughout those weekend hours that were once devoted to getting the car washed, getting the dog spayed, changing the refrigerator filters, and checking to see if the relief map of the continents that your daughter is making has finally dehydrated enough to keep Asia from bleeding into Europe. Most infuriating of all, those guys look pretty darn cute in their Gap pants and Tommy Bahama shirts at an hour when most of us moms still look like we've spent the night sleeping upside down like bats.

It's true. Golf takes up a lot of time and it can devour your weekend like a fox ravages a henhouse. When there is a lot on her plate, a woman will usually eat her vegetables before dessert, first things first, but that's not so with some men. Given the opportunity, many men will pass over the squash (cleaning out the garage) and go straight for the coconut cream pie (golf) without a second thought. For the person left at home, seeds of resentment can build. So what's the answer?

Find a middle ground. If he plays on Saturday morning and you can tear yourself out of bed, then put a cap over that bat hair and join him. After your round, help him tackle the home projects. If you have kids, let your husband play one day while you watch the youngsters, with the understanding that the following Saturday, it's your turn on the tee box.

Hire a babysitter. If your children are old enough, bring them along to the golf course. There are numerous options that will work if you are flexible and creative. What won't work is to deny your man—or yourself—time on the links. Everyone needs a break, and golf is an excellent outlet. In a busy life, playing every Saturday may not be realistic—but when you can "swing it," it's something to look forward to all week long.

Though I have, on occasion, employed the "Sunday Afternoon Sneak," I still don't play golf as often as my husband does. As much as I'd like to shoot par, I have other commitments and responsibilities that usurp my practice time—but that's my choice. I allocate my time in a way that makes me feel balanced and productive; my husband does too. He continues his Saturday Sneak on a regular basis, gathering with his buddies and colleagues for male bonding on the links, and I try not to begrudge him the time.

Perhaps his need for a weekend round (or two) is programmed into his DNA—perhaps not. Either way, he is more relaxed—and more supportive of my own golf outings and other events—when I let him vanish like David Copperfield for several hours every Saturday.

"PLAYING WITH THE BOYS"

So when your man is gone on his Saturday Sneak, what does he do? How does a friendly round among men differ from the typical non-competitive female golf outing? It differs *a lot!* Girls create a no-stress environment for each other. Gals may be flexible with scoring and rules when they're accompanied by a new dufferette learning the game. They offer encouragement; when a shot goes awry, they remind one another that they're playing "for fun." Girls like to chat; they sip Gatorade, water, and diet soda along the course. And though there are exceptions, they usually forgo the post-round drinks, quickly rushing off to other commitments once the game is over.

Men are altogether different. When men play the game, they're competitive. Although they are sportsmanlike, they do not offer each other a "you can do it" pep-squad cheer at the tee box. Instead, they bet cash they can beat one another and try their best to do so. They play by the book, talk very little, and are usually very focused on their game. A new player in their group does not get any favors; he's likely losing and buying the beer. Men might smoke cigars on the course, sending puffs of gray exhaust into the sky like Native Americans releasing smoke signals—somehow turning a simple golf outing into a primitive male-bonding experience.

Post round, the boys relax. They have drinks and burgers in the clubhouse S-T-R-E-T-C-H-I-N-G the leisure time like Plastic Man until finally they must report home to clean the garage or face a month without sex from a resentful wife (who may be late for her own tee time).

When I play with the guys, whether with just my hubby or with him and friends, the dynamic is different. The dissimilitude is intangible, but it is there. I am welcomed because they respect me as a person, though they may not necessarily consider me a competitor. Whether I shank a hit or crush a 165-yard drive down the middle of the fairway, most men are eerily silent. (My husband is the exception, offering constructive criticism and a detailed swing analysis with every poor shot, and abundant kudos with most great hits.)

Men assume most female golfers are hackers. They don't perceive us as a threat. If we're good, we hear crickets; they fastidiously concentrate on their own rounds to avoid getting beaten by a girl.

When I made a hole-in-one back in 1998, my husband could not have been more shocked had I walked on the moon. As my ball dropped onto the green and trickled down into the hole, he stood silent, mouth agape. He looked at me, glanced back at the green, and looked at me again. Then, reality set in. He blurted, and I quote, *"Holy sh**! My hacker wife just made a hole-in-one!"*

Later, I asked him about his gracious comments.

"You didn't think I could do it. You don't think I'm a very good player, do you?"

"No. I-I-I dunno," he stuttered. "Well, actually, a hacker is statistically more apt to make a hole-in-one than a scratch golfer."

Really. What a pat on the back. Thanks, Honey.

You'd think he could have thrown me a bone. But instead of saying, "Way to go!" he basically told me my ace was a fluke. Of course all hole-in-ones have a little help from the Luck Bug, but between you and me, I think my husband was a wee bit jealous of my eagle, and saying I lacked skill made him feel better about his par.

Sure, I was a hacker, but most golfers are. The majority of us do not play consistently enough to be competitive. Half the people who say they golf fall into the category of duffer. So we shouldn't be intimidated playing with the boys. Although they may not exhibit the primordial grunts and break out the cigars, they may genuinely enjoy your company, even if they don't say so. If you know the rules and get in some practice, you can hold your own—and you might even beat them. Tee it up with the boys when the opportunity presents itself. Have fun. Your female presence may be the breath of sweet air that makes them swear off stogies forever.

WHAT IRRITATES MEN MOST

I've discovered many behaviors that irritate men on the golf course, communicated by grumbling, icy stares, and reprimands. Here are the top vexations from the conglomerate male maw:

Excessive chatter. "Why is it women must make golf a 'social' event, talking about everything between each shot and sometimes between each putt? Quiet!"

"Women have the ability to talk in depth about meaningful topics anywhere in the world. A golf course is not the place for this."

Pace of play. "Learn to play ready golf—always be thinking about your next shot and be ready to play when it's your turn."

"Slow and good is bad enough; slow and bad is intolerable. If you've already reached double par on a hole, pick up and go to the green."

Ignorance of Etiquette. "My biggest irritation is ... women not knowing etiquette ... when to hit, who tees off first, who putts next."

"Be aware of everybody's putting line."

The Golf Cart. "My biggest irritation is over the issue of driving the golf cart properly."

"Proper placement of the cart on the course is an art, and when to move during the natural flow of play is a science. Of course, long-time golfers understand the nuances of where to park the cart at different points on the course and when to go or stop. A few examples:

"As a general rule, golf course superintendents get a little annoyed when they see two of the four tires of the cart touching the green. (Bad placement.)

"It's also a little frustrating to hear the brake pedal pop and the gas pedal hit the floorboard right in the middle of your backswing. (Bad timing.)

"I know my playing partners love to see the cart cruising the fairway thirty yards in front of them as they look up at the green when they've addressed the ball. (Not paying attention.)

"I love it when my cart is parked on the other side of the fairway and my wife and I are both standing on the same side and I need a new club. (Not sure how that happens.)"

Don't drive like granny. I've been with many a friend who inched the cart at a tortoise's pace. You don't have to be Mario Andretti, but you do need to drive the cart at a respectable pace. Yes, I know the tortoise beat the hare in the end, but the hare had time for two bathroom breaks and a visit to the snack bar before the back nine.

Crazy Speak. "It's a PAR-3, not a 3-PAR. This absolutely drives me crazy!"

"Every single woman I've played with asks me the same exact question about ten times a round: 'What am I doing wrong?'"

"Don't ask for swing advice from your significant other—that's almost always a recipe for disaster, and they are likely no more qualified than you are."

That's the gist. A few gents had an odd irritation here and there, but these main categories cover the bases. Once you finish this book, you'll know better what to do—and not to do—on the golf course. Primarily, learn the rules, keep up the pace, and play your game. I like how the last gentleman says your significant other is "likely no more qualified than you." His comment reveals that male golfers are fallible too. Men breach etiquette. Men shank shots. Still, many of them have been playing longer than us gals—like teabags, they are steeped in tradition and game know-how.

Be respectful of others. As you improve, you will want the same courtesy afforded you.

Oh … and do your best to leave Grandpa's Noodle ball on the course when you come across it. Whatever you do, don't pick it up!

GOLF FASHION—OR LACK THEREOF

As Vicki Iovine says, men "look pretty cute in their Gap pants and Tommy Bahama shirts." I agree. Not only do they look great, but golf is a sport perfectly tailored to the average man's wardrobe.

With the exception of a few suits, my husband's entire wardrobe is made up of golf-appropriate apparel. He has tons of khaki slacks, Dockers, and Bermuda shorts. His Polo collection encompasses collared shirts in every shade of the rainbow. He has Tommy Bahama shirts he wears to work, for a night on the town, and on the course. It's perfect!

Not only do they look great and feel comfortable, but men can practically fall right out of their cars onto the course; all they need to do is change their shoes. They don't have to spend a dime on golf attire, and their options are plentiful when deciding what to wear. It couldn't be easier.

It isn't so simple for us girls. I've fallen out of my car onto the golf course, but it wasn't because I was dressed for my round and ready to play. Instead, the heel of my stiletto caught on the door sill as I stepped onto the pavement. It wasn't pretty ... and neither are my golf clothes.

My wardrobe is made up of everything *but* Dockers and collared shirts. Seven jeans? Yep. A cute BEBE tank? Got it! A pencil skirt and strappy sandals? You bet. My closet has everything I need for a hot date, a business meeting, a cocktail party, or a day at the zoo. Can I wear any of it on the golf course? No way.

What to wear on the course seems so elementary—and it is for men—but women face quite a predicament. We can scrounge up four-year-old shorts and a company-issue Polo—and look so-so on the links—or sink some serious cash into ladies' golfwear we'll use only when on the course.

I don't know about you, but I like to look sharp, whatever I'm doing. (Even when falling out of a car, proper attire is important. I may have looked a bit surprised as I straightened my skirt and brushed gravel off my knees, but my shoes were just off the Nordstrom rack … so I'm sure I still looked pretty snazzy to those who witnessed my tumble.) Golf is no exception. Look good, feel confident, play well. It makes perfect sense. So just buy some golf clothes, right?

Sure, if "Greenback" is your middle name. If you haven't looked lately, golf attire is *expensive*. Wow! There are some cute clothes available for female players—soft skorts (now with pockets!), cute dri-weave Polo shirts, stylish jackets, and hats—but they ain't cheap. It may be worth a sizable investment if you plan to play the game on a regular basis, but if you're just starting out, consider investing in a few things you can wear over and over.

Pick colors that coordinate well with items you may already have. I suggest checking places like Old Navy for basics like shorts, then shopping for a few nice tops you can wear again and again. Polo has great golf attire for women. Nike has nice stuff too. I'd advise selecting sporty and classic over anything trendy. Keep in mind that if you pay $150 dollars for a pair of jeans, you'll likely wear them several times a week and get your money's worth. But you won't get the same bang for your buck spending $150 on a golf ensemble, unless you invest in something that will last for several seasons.

As far as golf shoes, you have two options. If you're on a tight budget, seek out some comfortable, neutral-colored shoes you can wear with a variety of outfits. Or, if you have a bigger pocketbook, buy golf shoes in lots of colors, to go with every outfit. There are many cute options available, and you know the old saying: "A girl can never have too many shoes." I'm absolutely positive that refers to golf shoes.

Even with a closet full of golf attire, women still have a harder time making the transition from the daily grind to the golf course and back. I have a friend, a corporate attorney, who is a fabulous golfer. She plays with her (all male) colleagues on a regular basis—usually before the workday begins.

"Let's play first thing in the morning," the men always suggest. "It's so much easier than other times of the day."

"Easier for whom?" she says when recounting the conversation. "I have to pack a bag with the clothes I need for work and get my kids dressed, fed, and dropped at day care, all before I get to the course. I'm going a million miles a minute—and it still takes me several hours to get it all done."

Even without kids to worry about, men have a distinct advantage. Post round they can make a meeting in 15 minutes; they just have to drive to the office. The khakis and collared shirts are considered "business casual" by most companies. After a morning of golf, a woman needs way more time to get to her desk.

"The guys are office-ready," my friend says. "I, on the other hand, have messy hair, or worse, a hat-head ring. I need a suitcase—with work clothes, a hairdryer, a curling iron, makeup—to make the transition to the office. And then they wonder what took me so long."

Who decided what we're supposed to wear on the golf course anyway? I don't think any females were involved in that process. We ladies must recreate our wardrobe to be course appropriate; in fact, the only thing we *don't* have to worry about is our underwear. However, while most new male golfers have a golf-ready wardrobe, they do need to keep in mind their choice of undergarment (boxers or briefs). Why? Tradition states that if a man fails to hit a ball past the ladies' (red) tee on his drive, he must take his next shot with his pants around his ankles.

I've witnessed this once, and it wasn't pretty. (Now, if I could pick which guys would shank the shot, it might make the game quite interesting.) Still, I'm glad girls don't have this tradition. We already have a lot to think about to look good on the green. If you're serious about your game and need golf clothes—*Wahoo!*—you now have an excuse to go shopping.

COURSE FARE

Just as with golf apparel, women clearly do not have much input into what vittles are available on the course. Hot dogs, chips, candy bars, beer, soda, and sugary sports drinks are the standard offerings. On occasion you may come across a dry turkey and Swiss, or a granola bar, but overall, the fare on a golf course is the nutritional equivalent of the spread at a birthday party. The foods I spend my whole week avoiding (and tell my kids not to eat) are in abundance on the links. Where is the Odwalla juice? Where are the Luna bars and veggie sandwiches? Is anything organic?

I have tried to stay healthy, even tucking a little baggie of baby carrots into the pocket of my golf bag, but after nine holes in the hot sun, a sweaty bag of warm vegetables does not do it for me. I've brought along trail mix and dried fruit, and I've seen a friend nibble rice cakes between holes, so it *is* possible to avoid the cart concessions and maintain a healthy diet. But it's also no fun at all. (And remember this: Some snacks—and baby carrots qualify—can make quite a crunching sound, so be careful when you nosh on noisy snacks. You don't want to distract others with your Doritos, apples, or anything else.)

Imagine this scenario: You've had a tough hole. You missed several swings in the bunker and eventually took a snowman—an 8—on the hole. You're hot, tired, and feeling manqué. Perhaps you need a snack to boost your blood sugar. Trying to be healthy, you retrieve the apple you brought from home. Just as you are about to take a bite, the "cart tart" pulls up with her plethora of goodies. The others in your group—all men—rush over for ice-cold beer and snacks.

"Honey, ya want anything?" calls your partner. "A beer? A frozen Snickers?"

What are you going to do? Seriously, you're going to cave. I did. Any honest gal with taste buds will tell you a smidge of chocolate can work wonders—satisfy a craving, ward off PMS, even relieve stress. And a beer with a lime slice sounds so much better than the tepid water in your sports bottle.

To succeed with any diet, Dr. Phil recommends creating a "no-fail" environment. Unfortunately, the golf course is not such a place. You can whiff a shot—and cheat on your diet—within minutes. Unless you have Teflon-coated willpower, you'll need to resign yourself to giving in to the frozen candy bar. Heck, golf is supposed to be fun, after all. I try to maintain a healthy diet, but most people will tell you balance is important too. So I indulge in course fare when I'm playing the links. And *sometimes*,

The Five Things Your Man Wants You to Know On the Golf Course

1. Be ready to play
2. Cut the chitchat
3. Don't slow people down
4. Keep track of your own score
5. Be confident and stand tall

the frozen candy bar is the highlight of my day.

Not long ago, I was munching on just such a chocolaty treat while my husband teed off on a par-3. He hit a great shot, and his ball sidled up on the green, close to the pin. As we walked back to the cart to drive to my tee box, a little old man passed us as he was walking by on a path that trailed past our hole.

"Make a hole-in-one and show him up," he said to me, with a wink.

I smiled and winked back. "I've done that before. He hates it."

LIGHT IT UP

Men have a history with the game of golf. Many boys grew up playing golf with their fathers; many retirees spend most every day at the country club chasing the little white ball. But even with the growing female contingent, there are still few ladies on the course. (At a company golf tournament I played with my hubby, I was one of only two women—and there were 70 men!) If the guys stare or are rude, forgive them. I think sometimes they forget women have as much right to play the links as they do.

Along with the right to swing the club comes a responsibility to know the rules and follow them. Do so. Be sensitive to etiquette. You don't need to tiptoe around the course, nor do you need to be a scratch golfer, but you do need to pay attention and engage in the game. Have fun; that means grab frozen Snickers if you want, and even bring some stogies for your girlfriends. I'm sure very soon there will be tell-tale puffs of female bonding floating skyward around the green long after the men have returned home to tackle that "honey-do" list.

9

ATTITUDE,
AWARENESS, AND
SNAKES

*If you are going to throw a club, it is important to
throw it ahead of you, down the fairway, so you
don't have to waste energy going back to pick it up.*

— Tommy Bolt

"THE DAY IS perfect," I say. A round of golf with friends, clear skies, a light breeze—what more could a person ask for? Nothing could spoil this day.

"Yep, it's pretty nice," agrees one of the guys in my group. We're playing on a company outing, so not only is the golf paid for, but it's a weekday and we're not in the office. It couldn't be better.

"Let's play that ball," says my husband, pointing to a white spot in the middle of the fairway. We're playing in a scramble tournament, so we make our way to where the best drive is located. My husband decides to hit first, and the other three of us stand behind, awaiting our turn. I have my club in hand, occasionally lifting it up and then letting it fall back to the ground, the shaft sliding through my fingers, in a thoughtless fidget to pass the time.

In a nanosecond, I see something flash in my peripheral vision.

Thunk! Smack!

"Celeste, are you OK?"

"Ugh. Yeah, I think." All of a sudden my right thigh is throbbing.

"What happened?"

"A golf ball just hit the shaft of my 3-wood and then tagged me on the leg. I had my club right by my head," I say, lifting the club to show them where it was when the ball hit.

Crunch! The graphite shaft flops over at a 90-degree angle.

"Oh my gosh, it broke the club," I say, in shock. Butterflies start to churn in my stomach as the thought of how fast the ball was traveling—and how close it had come to my head—begins to register.

"I didn't even see it coming," remarks one.

"I saw it for a split second, but it hit you before I could even open my mouth," says another.

"Did anyone hear a warning?" asks my husband. We all shake our heads no.

"You are so lucky."

"It freaks me out," admits my husband. "You could have died."

I want to cry.

Sure, with the exception of a big bruise on my leg, I'm no worse for wear. However, the thought of how close I had been to severe injury—or even death—rattles me. We had been in the middle of the fairway, another tee box or fairway nowhere in sight. No one yelled a warning. The ball had been inches from my head, and it broke the shaft of my club clear in half—a club which, incidentally, wasn't even mine. I had borrowed it from my sister-in-law to try out.

THE IMPORTANCE OF PAYING ATTENTION

You *must* pay attention on the golf course. My experience demonstrates that balls can strike you no matter where you are on the course, at any time. We never determined where the ball came from, but my guess is some really strong guy probably had a really bad slice and I was just really, really lucky to not get hit in the head.

Mistake No. 1: I was not paying attention. It was a tournament, so I was not keeping score. I was relaxed; my normal focus was not there. Instead of keeping an attentive eye on my surroundings, I was thoughtlessly fidgeting with my club. Yes, the ball was coming fast, and even had I seen it, I may not have been able to react quickly enough to get out of the way, but still, I should have been more focused on my surroundings.

Safety

Paying attention on the golf course keeps you and others from getting hurt. Don't walk too close when someone is swinging a club. After a ball is hit, follow its direction of flight. New golfers are notorious for some extremely poor "trick" shots, but remember, everyone is capable of a bad shot on occasion. Be alert and protect yourself. Keep your ears attuned to any warnings of "Fore!" or "Watch out!" It's all common sense, but it's worth repeating. A golf cart can't protect you, nor will a tree provide adequate coverage. Nothing replaces proper awareness. Nothing. And even if you have been crowned Ms. Attentive Universe, unfortunate events may still occur.

Another risk is lightning. In Colorado, summer thunderstorms are the norm. Almost every afternoon, dark clouds and rain roll in, often bringing lots of thunder and lightning. This is not golfing weather. If you are engaged in a round and foul weather blows in, take note. Is it just a passing rain squall or a thunderstorm? Some rain is nonthreatening and will pass quickly. A thunderstorm, on the other hand, can be life-threatening, especially if you're standing mid-fairway with a metal club in your hand.

Be smart about play. There are risks on a golf course. Risk is inherent in most everything—but don't take unnecessary chances. Live your life and play your game; just be aware and safe.

Club selection and course awareness

Paying attention may or may not save your life, but it will definitely help your golf game.

Imagine this: You have had a great hole and need only a short chip to the green and a one-putt for a possible birdie. You are too far away to use a pitching wedge, so you pull out your 9-iron and take a solid swing. The ball soars over the green, over the course fence, and out into the road.

"What club did you hit?" asks your boy-friend.

"I hit my nine," you say, just as shocked as he is at your powerhouse swing.

"Are you sure you didn't hit your six?" he asks, skeptically.

After closer inspection, you realize you did hit your 6-iron. Six ... nine, they look so similar. It's an honest error, right? Sure it is—but you just messed up your score and lost a favorite ball. Bye-bye birdie.

In addition to making the proper club selection, general awareness is also a must. Know where the hazards are, where the ground might be under repair, and where you are not allowed to drive the golf cart. Making note of these important details will keep you out of trouble—both with regard to your game and the ranger.

R-E-S-P-E-C-T

The right attitude can make or break your golf game. On the course you must respect yourself and other players at all times. Why? Because it's the right thing to do. Why else? Because there's a strong mind-body connection that can influence play.

Respect for Others

You should always be courteous. Most people pay a lot of money to play golf, and some are very serious about their game. If you are chatting endlessly or playing slowly, you are disrespecting others—perhaps foiling a great drive or backing up the pace of play for several foursomes. Be aware of how your voice might carry to another group. If the game is backed up, you may be waiting behind other players. If they have already teed off but are still on the fairway, don't hit until they are out of range. Not only will you put them in jeopardy if you hit up into them, but it's just plain rude. (I've had players hit into my group in an attempt, I presume, to hurry us along. Most of the time, I've been waiting for others in front of me and have had nowhere to go. Their "pushing" tactics flustered me and made me downright angry.) If they're on the tee box, give them some room. Don't drive your cart right up behind them. Stop short. The noise of the golf cart and your conversation will surely distract them. Take a break. Keep your conversation low. Observe the Golden Rule and treat others the way you want to be treated.

Respect for yourself

Respect for yourself falls into the category of the mental aspect of the game. Your attitude and what you tell yourself will make or break you—in golf and in life. Golf can be trying at times; you have to keep a healthy perspective and focus on the positive aspects of the game. When the going gets tough, remember:

• Be proud of yourself for attempting and learning the sport.

• Keep your head up and a smile on your face.

• What you focus on matters.

Be proud. Not long ago I organized a golf outing for the women at my church. The announcement of when we would play and other details ran in the Sunday program for three weeks. I also had a table set up after services for that same period of time, to answer any questions and encourage sign-ups. Several women came by to say they would love to play but then gave me their excuses for declining:

"Oh, I'm not very good. I don't want to embarrass myself."

"I really like golf, but I haven't played in ages."

"I'm not good enough to play in a group. You are all probably really good, huh?"

"No! No!" I'd tell them. "We're beginners playing. That's the whole point, to get the girls together in a no-stress atmosphere. Come play with us. We'd love to have you." But almost none could be persuaded. Out of a 1,500-member congregation, just eight women signed up—and two failed to show the day of the round. So, including me, we had seven women. Seven. How sad—but how fun for those who showed up.

I believe there is a misconception that if you're going to play golf, you must be a naturally gifted athlete. This is *not* the case. All beginners pretty much suck. Very few women step up to the red tees and par a hole on their first (or tenth) try. It takes time and practice.

So back to my first point: Be proud of yourself for taking a swing at it. You are one of the few women brave enough to get out there on the links. And inevitably, the ones who pass up the chance miss a very good time. The small group from church had a fabulous time. None of us were scratch golfers, but all of us had fun and even scored a few birdies, as well.

Keep your head up and smile. OK, so you're on the course but frustrated as all get-out. You've been in the sand trap repeatedly, and your score is downright humiliating. Don't quit! If at all possible, remind yourself that it's just a game and you're learning. Stand tall. Inner dialogue is key; if you give up mentally or berate yourself, you'll probably play poorly. Keep trying your best—the instant you're ready to quit, you'll have the shot of your life.

If you can't bear to keep score, put a ☺ for the holes you play well and a ☹ for the holes that aren't so great. At the end of the day, you won't have a big ugly number staring at you, just happy faces. And if you have more sad faces than happy smiles? Just flip your scorecard and turn those frowns upside down. Now you have more smiles! Remember, when you're learning, your score is irrelevant. Why frustrate yourself?

Focus matters. Your mind is a powerful tool; when you focus your energy, your game will follow. Inner dialogue is key. Consider the following inner conversations and their results:

"Oh my gosh, I'm never going to be able to hit over that water."

"Yes, you will. Just focus on the fairway. Don't look at the pond."

"But the water looks too far. I'll never be able to clear it."

"You can do it. You've cleared that distance ten times today."

"OK. I don't think I can, but I'll try."

Where do you think the ball went? Straight into the water, as if pulled by a strong magnetic force. She had already given up. Her focus was on her fear—not the fairway. I've found that if you focus fearfully on any hazard, your ball will be drawn to it like fans to a television camera.

Inner dialog two:

"There's water on this hole. Oh well, I can clear it, no problem."

"Are you sure? I hate the water."

"Yeah, but I can clear it. I've had drives farther than this at least ten times today."

Do I even need to tell you that she cleared the water? Of course she did. You knew her swing would be good because she believed in herself. You should too. A positive attitude increases your odds for success.

Contact is good. This was my motto when I was learning to play the game. Connecting with the ball and making forward progress down the fairway is what matters. If it scuttles along the ground or ricochets off a tree onto the fairway, go with it. Don't be too hard on yourself. Remember, there are no pictures on the scorecard (and sometimes only smiley faces).

Be gentle with yourself, but make no excuses. When I was learning to cook, my husband could have played Frisbee with my meatloaf, but I didn't care. I didn't say, "Well, I used a cake pan and forgot to adjust the cooking time." I just laughed and tossed him the phonebook to call for Chinese food. Mistakes don't humiliate us, they teach us. Next time we know what not to do, and things turn out better. Learn from your mistakes and keep trying. A bad round of golf or a bad meal does not define you. Above all, respect yourself. You—and your golf game—will be the better for it.

ENCOUNTERING WILDLIFE

My husband, Pete, and I are on a golf vacation in Arizona with our good friends Brent and Carolyn. As we play each hole, we can't help but notice the "Beware Rattlesnakes" signs along the periphery of the course.

"I don't need to find that ball," I tell my husband, after hitting out-of-bounds. "I'd rather take a penalty than meet a rattlesnake."

On the next hole, the guys tee off first, then Carolyn and I hit from the red tees. Both of us have nice drives, but Carolyn's ball rolls over the crest of the fairway and disappears out of sight.

"Nice drive!" I tell her. "I wish I'd hit my ball that far."

Pete and I zip over to my ball, and I take my second shot, still a bit bummed that my drive had fallen short of my expectations. Then we're off to find Pete's drive. As we round the top of the fairway and make our way down the hill, we see a huge snake. It's crossing the fairway and is very close to a golf ball. The sight of the slithering serpent gives me the heebie-jeebies. I pull my feet back into the cart.

"Is that your ball?" I ask Pete.

"Nope, it's Carolyn's."

Then, in my most supportive and concerned-for-my-friend voice, I say, "I'm sure glad that's not *my* ball."

When you play golf, you will encounter wildlife. You may hear the buzz of nearby cicadas, see dragonflies zoom past, or have gnats fly up your nose. Depending on where you live and/or where you are playing, you may meet some species that are a little more dangerous and creepy than others. While playing in Florida, an alligator—albeit a small alligator—was lurking in a water hazard. I'm fine with alligators in the zoo, but on a fairway with me? Not so much. I've seen lots of snakes and even stepped on one in the rough. I've seen big lizards, huge spiders, and been chased by one very, very mean goose that adopted my ball. A brush with the not-so-nice species of animals (and mosquitoes) sometimes disrupts my game focus. When I'm contemplating the alligator or guarding against the goose, I have stopped thinking about my club selection and shot strategy.

At other times, I have encountered nicer, more elusive wildlife that quickly scurries away, leaving me feeling as if I'm playing golf on *Wild Kingdom*. Sighting coyotes, foxes, deer, rabbits, squirrels, ducks, fish, and prairie dogs makes the round all the more fun. Gopher sightings trigger clips from *Caddyshack* in my mind's movie reel. Sunshine, fresh air, and exercise are great—throw in a few wildlife sightings and you have a day to treasure.

Still, however much fun they are to see, most animals you encounter on a golf course will be wild, so heed these precautions to make sure you stay safe:

Obey all posted signs and use caution with snakes and other wildlife. The course we were playing warned of snakes, and we saw them. If the signs are up, the animals are there. Though you may encounter wildlife on a fairway, the probability of running into a snake (or links-loving bear) is even higher if you're poking around out-of-bounds.

If you do encounter an animal, stay away from it. Just like mom used to say in the department store: "Look, but don't touch." If you leave them alone, they will likely leave you alone.

Focus on your game, not taking a great picture. If a string of baby goslings is trailing across the fairway toward a pond on hole 11, take a moment to watch them. Don't grab your camera and attempt to snap the next cover shot for *National Geographic*; this will take time away from your round, disrupt the game, and worse, potentially annoy the mommy goose. You don't want that, believe me!

Don't wear perfume when you play golf. Please, please wear deodorant, but avoid heavy scents. Though I smell quite nice when I spritz on a flowery eau de cologne before a round, the bees, flies, and bugs think I smell great too. It's hard to focus on your game with bees buzzing around your shoulders as you try to swing, and bugs nibbling your knees as you putt. Save the perfume for after your round. (You'll need it more then, anyway.)

Be aware of your surroundings. Know where you are hitting and avoid areas that could be dangerous. You wouldn't want to hit an animal with your ball, nor have one come after you if you did.

DON'T BE A "GIRLY MAN"

OK, I admit it. When the goose chased me, I screamed. I not only screamed, but I also dropped my club, threw my hands in the air, and ran away as fast as I could.

"What the heck are you doing?" asked my husband.

"That goose was chasing me."

"I can see that. But it was a *goose*."

"Well, it was a *mean* goose. It was sticking its neck out and hissing at me. I think it was going to bite me."

"No it wasn't," he laughed.

"Um, yeah, I'm pretty sure it was."

"Well, you have to go back and get your club."

"I'm not getting my club."

"You can't leave it there."

"Will you go get it?"

"No!"

"Please? I'll owe you one."

"Fine," he says, walking towards my abandoned club and the mafia goose. "Sometimes, you're such a girl."

While this incident is funny, in hindsight, I hate how I reacted. It was such a "girly" thing to do, and in this one instance I use "girly" in its least flattering connotation, as in a third-grade screamer fleeing from a playground bee. That is so not me. I believe in women and the wonderful qualities we possess; we are strong, talented, intelligent, loving, and resilient. If you're a female golfer, one might also assume you are confident, competent, and brave—not the type to be rattled by sharing the course with more experienced male golfers—or even snakes with rattles.

Respect, Safety and Attitude

R egard
E veryone
S o
P laying
E vokes
C ourteous
T ransactions

S taying
A lert
F osters an
E xample like
T iger Woods!
Y es!!!!

A lways
T ry to
T ee up with
I nspired
T enacious
U nequivocal
D etermination and
E nthusiasm!

Still, the goose caught me off guard. While that's no excuse, it's all I can say. You may, on occasion, be caught off guard by an animal on the course. If so, try not to scream, and definitely do *not* drop your club. If you encounter a poisonous snake, you may need your club to fend off the slithery reptile (if you've aggravated it) and you don't want to have to go back for it. Calmly and quickly relocate. You could be a scratch golfer, but if you howl in fear and sprint across the golf course chased by a ground squirrel, my guess is the others in your group will consider you to be "girly."

Develop mental toughness. It is not just your game, but your attitude and the way you handle yourself that will win you respect on the golf course. You can handle the snakes without screeching. You can deal with PMS cramps without complaining. You can deal with the heat, the bugs, and the crappy shots. Just play. If the beverage cart is out of Diet Coke, oh well. If a storm blows in and you have to take a rain check, stay positive. Demonstrate to other players that you're not only a decent golfer, but a well-rounded, confident gal who is a lot of fun to be with. Which, of course, you are.

Having a good time and staying safe on a golf course requires that you pay attention to your game and surrounding environment. Make prudent decisions, but above all, remember that golf is just a game. You never want to risk bodily injury (or death), whether the result of a misdirected ball, a lightning strike, or a wild animal. Golf is a great game. It can be relaxing, full of challenges, and fun. It also offers a host of opportunities to learn about yourself.

I've learned that a positive focus and attention to detail transcend the game of golf and help me in all areas of life. I've also learned I can encounter a snake or an alligator without getting a hiccup in my swing. It's all mental. And yes, I'm still "mental" about geese, but I'm making progress.

10

GETTIN' SERIOUS

Lessons, Handicap, and League Play

My handicap? Woods and irons.
— Chris Codiroli

"SO ARE YOU excited to play today?" my husband asks as I pull a pink Polo shirt over my head and start to apply sunscreen to my face.

"Actually, I'm kinda nervous."

"That's OK. It's good for you to get out of your comfort zone. You'll learn a lot by playing with these ladies."

"I know. I just don't want to embarrass myself."

This was my first day playing in a women's golf league. Though it was designed to be a non-competitive league, I knew some of the ladies

217

were longtime leaguers and really good golfers. I was afraid I wouldn't be able to keep pace, that I would make an ass of myself, hack up the course, and post the worst score in the group.

"Tell them if you shoot a hundred you'll be lucky," advises my husband. "That'll take some pressure off."

"Well, we're only playing nine."

"OK, so tell them you hope to shoot a fifty," he says.

"I just want to play my best today," I tell him. "I don't want them to think I suck."

"You probably won't have your best round today. Nerves can throw off anyone's game; just realize it's a learning process and try to relax."

When I get to the course, I find the two other ladies in my group are much older than I am; in fact, one could have been my grandmother. I introduce myself. "I'll follow your lead today," I tell them. "This is my first day playing in the league. You'll have to help me out if I have a question."

"No problem," they say in unison, my personal cheerleading duo.

"I'll be lucky if I break fifty today," I warn one of the ladies.

"Don't worry," she assures me, "we play a lot, but we're not very good either. We just come out here for fun."

She wasn't kidding. These two ladies, bless their hacking hearts, were two of the slowest golfers I had ever played with. (I was thankful we went off the tee box last; at least we weren't holding up play for other groups.) One was a semi-decent player, the other was—and I say this in my most respectful, open-minded way— absolutely, positively horrible.

Per the rules of our league, the maximum score one might take on a hole is a 10. This woman took a 10 on *every* hole! But she had fun! She didn't care about her score, and she was a hoot to play with. Not only did she make me feel comfortable (compared to her, I felt I might have a chance on the pro circuit), but she was jovial and positive throughout her round. She kept trying, and despite some very crazy shots (off the cart, then off a tree, and into the rough), she stayed upbeat.

These two dainty duffers gave me a powerful reminder that it's not always about the score. It's about the game and the experience, putting yourself out there and just going for it, no matter what your skill level. I had waited several seasons to join this group, thinking I needed to be a better player before I joined a league. Now I see that reasoning is akin to losing weight before setting foot in a gym or cleaning the house before the maid arrives. It makes no sense. The way to get better is to *play*—and playing affords us many opportunities to improve our game, meet friends, and live life to the fullest, regardless of skill.

Since then I've signed up to play with ladies more on a par with my pace and skill level. While I learned a lot from those golf gals in terms of attitude and inspiration, I wanted golfers who would challenge me in terms of skill. I found them. Now I'm pushed to my limit most every time I play. But even on my bad days, I keep my head up. In this position, even if my score goes south, I still have the sun on my face.

A LESSON ON LESSONS

If you know the rules, etiquette, and have a positive attitude, you can survive a friendly game of golf without a ton of skill. The operative word here is *survive*; simply pick up your ball if the score count gets high and keep pace with the others, regardless of how many shots you take. Like many gals, you may delight in playing just three or four rounds a year with friends. Great! You're in good company.

If you want to take your game to the next level, crave a respectable game, or aspire to competitive play, you should take lessons. Lessons will help your swing technique, short game, speed control in putting, surviving the sand trap, and more. A rules clinic, a class on etiquette, or an on-course lesson may also be helpful.

If you have a particular area that needs work, a pro will gladly help you target that part of your game. Likewise, if you think your whole game could use some work, an instructor can take you step by step through the whole process, from your car to the last putt on 18. They won't teach you how to get out of a meeting early or find the perfect babysitter, but they can help with just about everything else.

You can choose from private lessons, semi-private instruction (two or three individuals), or group lessons. The cost is usually determined by how many people attend and how many lessons you take; generally, the larger the group, the lower your overall cost will be. Private lessons are more costly. A plethora of options are available at private and public courses or recreation centers. Check the Internet, the phone book, or call a local golf store for information on lessons. You should be able to connect with a pro in your area.

Find the right teaching style for you. It may take a few lessons, or instructors, to find a teaching style that works for you. I have tried both male and female golf instructors and have learned a lot from both.

You may feel more comfortable with a female instructor or be perfectly fine with a male teacher. The way I see it, golf instructors are like flavors of ice cream; you may find some you like better than others, but in the end they're all pretty good.

Get there early. Arrive at the course at least 20 minutes before your lesson. You'll want to allow ample time to park, get your clubs, and warm up before you meet with the instructor. If you have time to hit a bucket of balls and stretch prior to your lesson, that is ideal. You'll be doing yourself a disservice if you are late and start your lesson cold.

Like physicians, most golf instructors have busy schedules; they likely have other clients coming in after you, so they don't tend to appreciate or accommodate tardiness. If you have a lesson scheduled from 2:30 to 3:00, and you don't show until 2:40 and it takes you 10 minutes to warm up and get in the groove, you'll have 10 minutes of quality instruction time, even though you're paying for 30.

Practice what they preach. Another thing to consider is that lessons are a waste of money if you don't follow up with regular practice and play. Take lessons if you are serious about your game and have a strong desire to improve. You will make significant strides if you are sincerely dedicated to learning the game. This isn't to say that, if you take lessons in the summer and then don't play at all during winter, you'll forget everything, but you might forget some important pointers.

Don't let too much time pass between swings. Even in coldest climates there are options to keep your game "warm." Many cities have heated or indoor driving ranges where you can practice when there's snow on the ground outside. If winter weather has stalled your game and you have no place to practice, then it's time for a tropical vacation. Golf is great in Hawaii and Arizona in December! Be creative and the world will be your golf course.

ESTABLISHING A HANDICAP

According to *The Historical Dictionary of Golfing Terms* a handicap is "compensation in strokes assigned to players on the basis of their past and current performance, designed to enable players of different abilities to compete together on approximately equal terms." In league play, tournaments, and even friendly games, handicaps level the playing field.

It works like this: Let's say you normally shoot about a 95 for 18 holes and your handicap is 23. Your partner shoots an 80 on average; his handicap is an 8. When playing together with handicaps in effect, you will be allowed to deduct 23 strokes from your total score. Usually these strokes, also called "pops," are subtracted from your total score to give you a net total. The handicap strokes, often listed on a scorecard as small dots, are sometimes assigned according to the difficulty of each hole—the "handicap of the hole."

If you look at a scorecard, usually below where you write your name you will see a "par" listing. Beneath the par designation is usually the "handicap," with the difficulty of the hole indicated by a number from 1 to 18 (for 18 holes), the hardest hole being 1 and the easiest being 18. Handicap strokes may be assigned by hole, based on difficulty. If your handicap is 8, you will get eight strokes or dots. Your scorecard might look like this: (This example is for nine holes.)

Hole		1	2	3	4	5	6	7	8	9	
Black	71.1/126										
Blue	70.6/124										
Red	69.8/119										
Name #1											
Name #2											
Name #3											
Name #4											
Par		4	4	5	3	4	4	3	5	4	
Handicap		7	4	3	8	5	9	6	1	2	
(Dots, strokes, or pops)			•	••		•		•	••	•	

If you look at the dots, they are given for the more difficult holes, based on the assumption that you'll do better on the easier holes. If you shoot par on hole No. 2, your net total, after subtracting the dot given, would be a three. If you score an eight on the eighth hole (the hardest, with a handicap rating of 1), your net score would be a six, as you are given two strokes on that hole.

Overall, your net score will be the same as if you had deducted eight strokes from your total. Some courses' scorecards will have a place for you to subtract your handicap to produce the net score. In that case your scorecard might look like this:

Hole	14	15	16	17	18	IN	TOT	HCP	NET
Name/ Score	3	4	5	4	4	40	82	8	74

In this example, I'm showing just the back part of the scorecard to give you an idea how it might look. "IN" is the total for the first nine holes you just finished. "TOT" is the total score of both nines, your score for the entire round. "HCP" is your handicap; in this case, it's an 8.

"NET" is your net score for all 18 holes. Make sense? Handicaps level the playing field. If you have a handicap of 23 and your partner has a handicap of 8, in a normal round of golf he/she would blow you away, and that's no fun.

However, with handicap allowance, if you have a great day and shoot a 94 and your partner has an average game and shoots an 80, figuring in handicaps, you would win! Here's how: 94 minus a handicap of 23 is a net score of 71. A score of 80 with a handicap of 8 yields a net score of 72. Even though your partner is a more skilled player, based on what you usually score, you had the better day, so you win by one stroke. Now *that* is fun!

Get a GHIN number. An official handicap is required to participate in most leagues and tournaments, plus as just demonstrated, it can make a casual Sunday round more fun. So how do you establish a handicap? The first thing you need to do is get a GHIN number. Though there are other handicapping services, the GHIN (Golf Handicap Information Network) is the largest and therefore most prevalent in the United States. The GHIN system calculates your handicap based on your average scores and the course rating and slope of the courses you play. (The course rating and slope are the numbers listed next to the tee color on your scorecard.)

For example, in the first scorecard example the course rating and slope for the red tees is listed as: 69.8/119. This is basically the difficulty level of the course. Some courses will be easier, some harder; your total handicap will take into consideration not only your score but also the course difficulty, ensuring equality among golfers no matter where you play.

If you belong to a private course or club, you can usually just contact the pro shop to get a GHIN number set up. Some public courses also work with the GHIN system. If you don't have a home course you play, you can go to the GHIN Web site at www.GHIN.com, click on the listing for affiliated golf associations, and contact them directly. There is a small fee to establish a GHIN number.

Hit the links. Once you have a GHIN number, play some golf. After each round, enter your scores and appropriate course rating into the computer at the course you play. (If you need help with this, ask a staff member to walk you through the process.) You can also post scores on line through the www.GHIN.com Web site. Just go to the section entitled "Post On Line" and follow the prompts.

You will have to play several rounds to get a handicap index; typically, you'll need to post 10 nine-hole rounds or five rounds of 18 holes before your handicap is official. Then, as you keep playing and posting rounds, your handicap will evolve. You can sign up to receive e-mail updates of your handicap each month. This is an easy way to track your progress and ensure that you always have the most accurate handicap index.

Honesty is the best policy. As with all rounds of golf, be honest when recording your scores. Some unsportsmanlike players are thought to pad their handicap by recording scores that don't reflect their true capabilities. For example, if a player shoots a 78, but records an 83—he's inflating his handicap. The benefit? The player can then enter tournaments and easily beat others within a similar handicap bracket.

This is called "sandbagging," artificially inflating your handicap so you can win in competitive play. In my opinion, sandbaggers ruin competition for everyone. Even though they may take home a prize, they are true losers.

At the same time, when you are establishing your handicap, make sure you play out every hole. When I was establishing my handicap, I was discouraged with my scores.

"Why are you disappointed?" asked my husband. "That's about what you normally score."

"I know," I admitted. "I guess since it's going into a computer I wanted it to be a really low score."

"But you don't score really low. Your handicap should reflect how you play every day."

I knew my husband was right. If I recorded artificially low scores, I'd be paired with others beyond my skill range, and that wouldn't be fun either. Honesty is the best policy—always know the rules, score accurately, and truthfully record your scores. Nobody wants to play with a sandbagger or a cheat; have integrity and pride in your game, no matter what your handicap may be.

"Stand tall," says my husband. "You're making progress." Stand tall. That's good advice—good for your posture, good for your game, and great for your morale.

LEAGUE PLAY AND TOURNAMENTS

One way to take your game to the next level is to join a golf league. There are many types, from casual to extremely competitive, nine holes to 18 holes, executive groups, and so on. A league will instantly bring you into contact with lots of other golfers who love the game and play on a regular basis. One of the reasons I joined a league is so I would actually commit to playing every week. Previously, I might have played two rounds a week or gone two months without a round. I thought a league would help me stick to my golf program and facilitate consistency.

Leagues can be gender specific or coed. Most leagues require a membership fee, which generally covers administration costs and supplements the cost of any awards. Though they can be lumped with the membership fee, greens fees usually are paid separately.

Leagues meet at different times. Some play weekday mornings and afternoons; these leagues tend to attract retirees who have flexible schedules, work-from-home ladies with variable routines, and moms whose kids are in school. Evening and weekend leagues tend to attract a more career-oriented crowd. Eighteen-hole leagues usually include a demographic of women who are more serious about their game, and while nine-hole leagues can be very competitive, they also are more apt to comprise newer players who are not yet up to the challenge of a full 18 holes every week.

Different leagues have different rules and guidelines. Once you join, you'll probably be given a booklet with contact information for the course and league officers, rules, important dates, prizes, awards, etc. for your specific league.

When you play in a league, you'll need to have a handicap and a GHIN number. You'll use the GHIN number to properly track and record your scores as well as keep an up-to-date handicap index. Your handicap is used to group you with golfers of a comparable skill level. In my league, golfers are placed into flights based on their handicaps.

For example, one flight of golfers might have an "A" handicap player, a "B" handicap player, and a "C" handicap player. The "A" players are generally those with the lowest handicaps (best golfers), and the "C" players usually have higher handicaps. If you haven't established a handicap, you would generally play in the "rest of field," after other players have teed off, and/or you would play with a zero handicap (scratch golfer) until you had played enough rounds to post an official handicap.

What does this mean? It essentially means you will lose. If you generally shoot a 97 and you play with no handicap, you'll lose to other players who may shoot your same average score but have a 25 handicap working in their favor. Don't worry, though. Most leagues have a grace period to establish your handicap before handicap-based rounds kick in.

Even if you enter a league late or don't qualify for handicap events and prizes, join anyway. You will inevitably learn a lot about golf, improve your game, make new friends, and have a lot of fun—which is the whole point!

EQUITABLE STROKE CONTROL

One thing I really like when playing in a league is Equitable Stroke Control. Basically, the system is designed to keep any one horrible, no-good, very bad hole from skewing your overall handicap. For instance, if your overall handicap is a 40 or more, you might not take more than a 10 on any given hole. (These numbers vary from league to league *and* change with your handicap. As your handicap gets better, the maximum allowable score per hole will be lower.)

Still, for those days when you fall apart on a certain hole, this system can save your booty. And, like the lady in my league who took a 10 on every hole, there's an upside. First, there is a lot of room for improvement. And second? Not many women can honestly say they are always a perfect 10!

TOURNAMENTS

You gotta love a good old-fashioned golf tournament. When I lie in bed at night before a tournament, visions of goodie bags, box lunches, and shotgun starts dance in my head. Of course, there are many types of golf tournaments—competitive tournaments, group tournaments, and individual tournaments—with just about any format you can imagine: stroke play, match play, skins, you name it. Really, a whole book could be written on tournament types and formats. However, what I'm talking about (and the best type of tournament for a new golfer) is a charity golf tournament.

Charity tournaments. Charity tourneys abound. Usually, you can register individually or with a group to play in these events, so it's fun to round up a group of friends and make a day of it. Yes, you will typically pay an entry price higher than a typical greens fee, but the cost of your entry generally includes some sort of post-round meal, a giveaway bag filled with tees, balls, a snack, and perhaps a hat or t-shirt. Plus, the proceeds from your round will benefit the greater good. You can't beat that.

Part of what is so fun about a charity tournament is that it's usually a "no pressure" atmosphere. Many tournaments of this type are in a scramble format. Scramble may be what the cable company does to your HBO when you don't pay your bill, or the way you had your eggs for breakfast, but the golf-type scramble is when everyone hits, the majority picks the best shot of the group (usually a foursome), and everyone hits again from that spot. You take the best shot from each round of hits—so easy. If you have the drive of your life—*Yippee!*—the group will probably play your ball; if you shank the shot of your life, who cares? The group will just play someone else's ball.

Best-ball tournaments. Another type of tournament format is best ball. While best ball logically sounds like a scramble, they are not to be confused. In a best-ball format, everybody plays their own ball and then the group takes the best score on the hole. For example, if one player shoots a four on a hole, two have fives, and you shoot a nine, the group will take the four as their score for that hole. Again, it's always nice if you play well, but no real spin off your club if you don't.

Mulligans. Another reason tournaments are more relaxed is that you generally can buy mulligans. A mulligan is a "do-over" of a particular shot. For instance, if you drive your tee shot into a tree and it bounces back to wind up four feet in front of the tee box, you can use a mulligan and hit again. The money raised from buying mulligans usually goes right to the charity cause, so I'm happy to buy as many as they'll allow me to have.

Prizes. Many tournaments have awards. These generally include prizes for the team with the lowest overall score, longest drive, and closest to the pin. I am the proud recipient of a tournament award for best head covers. (Everyone just loves my chicken with the egg.)

There are often other silly tournament-specific awards you can win as well. At most charity tournaments there will be a chance to win a car if you have a hole-in-one on the specified hole. Usually they will have the brand-new, gleaming automobile parked near the tee box on the designated par-3. (Why a par-3? In case you didn't know—I didn't when I first started— virtually all hole-in-ones are recorded on par-3 holes. The distance for most all par-4 holes is too great to drive in a single shot.)

The sight of the car is generally enough to create a Pavlovian response in many golfers, and they'll start to salivate over the prospect of driving it home. To guard against humiliation, some may casually wipe the excess saliva from their face and thus ruin their chances for claiming the car. Here's the problem: the "slippery saliva swing" is never a good one. Inevitably, when it counts, your ball (or your club) will go flying in a direction you never knew it could. You might be disappointed at losing the car, which you could almost taste, but usually a cool drink will remedy the problem, and you can move on with your game.

After the day is over—and these events tend to take all day—you can relax with your friends post round. Food is usually provided, and drinks are always available at the bar. Many of these tournaments are followed by an auction—silent, live, or a combination of both—and then they pass out the awards. (This is done after the auction so you'll stick around and spend your cash.)

Generally these events are fun, with very little stress. If you want to put your six months of private lessons to the test, you can track down many competitive, high-stress tournaments through your local golf club. However, if you just want to relax, play the game with friends, and exercise your philanthropic swing, then a charity tourney may be just up your fairway.

GOLF SCHOOL

If you want rapid improvement in your game, have vacation time burning a hole in your pocket, and are willing to invest the money, consider going to golf school. There are many types of golf schools, from single-day instruction one-on-one with a golf pro, to week-long lessons in a group format and everything in between. There are more than 2,500 golf schools in the United States today, so with a little research you can find a school that fits your golfing needs, schedule, and price range.

Many golf schools are at luxurious resorts in locales such as California, Arizona, and Florida. It's wonderful to end a long day of golf tutelage with a five-star meal and a big comfy bed. A resort setting also provides many activities for any nongolfer traveling companions. If you want to spend the day at golf school, but your husband would rather lie by the pool and have a massage at the spa, then you might want to consider a bigger resort-based school. If you really just want to focus on your swing, and don't care much about amenities, there is a school to accommodate those needs as well.

I have a few suggestions to ease this sometimes overwhelming process, but with a little legwork, you can find a school that works for you.

Make a list of your requirements. What areas of your game do you want to focus on most? Do you learn best by yourself or in a group? How many days can you get away? What's your price range? Do you want a women-only school? Consider what matters to you, and get it on paper.

Plan ahead. With more than 2,500 options, you're going to need some time to do your research. First, ask for recommendations. Do you know someone who has attended golf school? What was their experience? What was the instruction style? What are their recommendations? Second, search the Internet. I like the Web site www.golfschoolinfo.com, but there are hundreds of good sites. Go to a search engine such as Google and type in "golf school" and a few other key words, such as the area you would like to go to, your home town, or the month you want to travel. See what links pop up and check them out. Third, request brochures from the schools you like best. Then, after reviewing the material, conduct phone interviews with the schools to narrow the list. There are many great schools; it's worth the time to find one that best meets your needs. Do your research.

Search for a great deal. If you are flexible with your time frame and want to save a few dollars, periodically scan the 'Net for special rates. Just like airlines, golf schools occasionally offer great deals, but often on short notice. If this appeals to you, be diligent. Consider recruiting a friend to attend with you; I've seen two-for-one deals pop up from time to time. If you can land one of these, you can split the cost.

Apply what you learn. Remember, as with lessons, if you return home

11 Tips for New Female Golfers

1. Have a positive attitude
2. Take lessons
3. Make time to practice
4. Buy the best clubs you can afford
5. Seek friends to golf with
6. Get a good babysitter
7. Lose the scorecard
8. Invest in cute golf clothes
9. Come to the course prepared
10. Laugh when you want to cry
11. If Tips 1-10 fail, take up tennis

and fail to apply what you have learned in regular practice and play, you may lose much of the benefit. Of course, the vacation and time off from work is nice in and of itself, but if you invest money and time in golf school, follow through on your swing and keep hitting the links when you get home.

CLIMBING THE LADDER

If you desire to take your golf game to the next level, there are many rungs you can climb up the ladder to par. Lessons, leagues, and golf school all are great options, and quality instruction cannot be overemphasized. Once you commit to advancing your game, stick with it. Play on a regular basis—even if it's just charity tournaments—any opportunity to swing the club, practice your putting, and improve your game is a good one.

Golf provides a fabulous opportunity for women. We have many qualities that enhance our aptitude for the game, but we must get out there and play. If becoming a great player is important to you, then keep at it. Find the time. Set goals and make the sacrifice. You will get there. And I'm willing to bet you'll turn a few heads doing it.

11

CONCLUSION

Golf is a day spent in a round of strenuous idleness.

— William Wordsworth

WITH EACH PASSING day, more and more women are taking a swing *From the Red Tees*. Whether playing with business associates, partners, or friends, we are a growing segment of the golfing population. And yet, there are gals who are reluctant to try the game because they feel they lack basic knowledge; they fear making a fool of themselves on the green, so they don't take the risk. The campus lie is, if you're a female golfer, you must be a natural for the game. This is so not true. Most women who pick up a club for the first time are not "naturals." But we can still make golf a part of our lives.

You don't have to be a scratch golfer to be a competitive player. With the handicap system, players of different abilities can engage in rounds together and have lots of fun. Sure, if you want to excel at the sport, regular practice and lessons are in order, but if you know the basic rules and etiquette, you can play a friendly round a few times a year and enjoy yourself.

Whatever your goals, remember to keep things in perspective when the ball doesn't break in your direction. You probably don't play enough to be so hard on yourself, and even if you do, I'm guessing you still don't have a private coach and sponsors counting on you to win a major event. Relax. It takes a lot of guts just to get on the green. Be proud of how far you have come, and realize that everyone, even Tiger and Annika, has days when they wish they could have played better.

I have days when I wish I could play better—and days I wish I could just get on the course. We are, after all, women with deadlines and appointments, laundry and lists; life conspires (on occasion) to usurp our golf game entirely. Well, the laundry can *always* wait. Just pick up a pack of underwear at Wal-Mart on the way home from the course.

Sick kids and doctor's appointments are not so easy to skirt. (Sigh.) We may have to skip our rendezvous with the links on occasion, for however much we love the game, some things in life are just more important than golf.

Focus on the experience of playing the game, not just your score. The opportunity for challenge and improvement, the chance for exercise and time with friends, big deep breaths of fresh air, and huge bites of frozen Snickers are what bring me back to the game—often in spite of my score. If you just focus on a number, you will miss a good part of the joy the game has to offer.

Girls, tee it high and let it fly. Just get out there and *play!* Bring your friends. If they're hesitant, give them a copy of this book; it'll provide the basic knowledge they need and the reassurance that we all whiff the ball sometimes.

I wish you clear skies, long drives, straight putts, and attractive bag boys. I wish you supportive friends, reliable babysitters, cute golf attire (with pockets), and friendly wildlife. I wish you more birdies than you can count and lots and lots of fun on the fairway. Enjoy the game. I can't wait to see you out there playing *From the Red Tees*.

INDEX

MY GOLF NOTES

_____
_____
_____
_____
_____
_____
_____
_____
_____
_____
_____
_____
_____
_____
_____
_____
_____
_____
_____
_____
_____
_____
_____
_____
_____
_____